PERSONALITY DEVELOPMENT FOR WORK

SIXTH EDITION

HAROLD R. WALLACE
Professor of Occupational & Educational Studies
Colorado State University
Ft. Collins, Colorado

L. ANN MASTERS
Administrator, Vocational Program Services
Nebraska Department of Education
Lincoln, Nebraska

K43
PUBLISHED BY
SOUTH-WESTERN PUBLISHING CO.
CINCINNATI   WEST CHICAGO, IL   CARROLLTON, TX   LIVERMORE, CA

ISBN: 0-538-11430-4
Library of Congress Catalog Card Number: 87-62249

1 2 3 4 5 6 7 8 RM 5 4 3 2 1 0 9 8
Printed in the United States of America

Preface

Success in the world of work is based not only on one's ability to perform the requirements of the position, but also on the ability of the worker to get along with others. *Personality Development for Work* is designed to help the new employee recognize the important role that personality plays in the work environment. The text focuses on the personality factors essential to good human relationships in the workplace.

RESEARCH FOR THE TEXT

The chapters that focus on work adjustment and interpersonal relationships are based on thorough review of recent research and theory development in modern psychology. This helped to ensure that the ideas presented are valid and realistic in the work world. A comprehensive review of studies about employer expectations and causes of failure on the job is the foundation for helping students develop the personality type that contributes to job success. Understanding and applying this information allows a new worker to make adjustments necessary to fit in and become a productive member of a working team.

THE CRITICAL PERSONALITY FACTORS

Personality is important on the job because people do not have the opportunity to choose their supervisor and coworkers. Stress, conflict, and miscommunication in the workplace can often cause difficulties. Positive personality characteristics can help a worker to *adjust*—to get along and fit in. Negative personality traits can hamper or prevent critical adjustments. This book helps the worker assess his or her personality to find out what changes and improvements must occur in preparation for successful employment.

Success-related personality factors can be identified because there has been so much research on the subject. The results of this research consistently point out several common, logically related "clusters" of personality traits. All of the most important traits fit into one of fifteen categories. The major objective of this text is to help the individual understand and develop his or her personality in all fifteen areas.

The fifteen categories of greatest importance to success in employment are:

1. Ambition
2. Cooperation and helpfulness
3. Adaptability and resourcefulness
4. Consideration and courtesy
5. Independence, showing initiative
6. Concern for quality of work and accuracy
7. Carefulness, alertness, and perceptiveness
8. Pleasantness, friendliness, and cheerfulness
9. Responsiveness; the ability and willingness to follow directions
10. Perserverance, patience, and tolerance
11. Emotional stability, poise, and the ability to use good judgment
12. Neatness and orderliness in appearance and manner
13. Dependability, punctuality, responsibility, and reliability
14. Efficiency, speediness, and productivity
15. Dedication, loyalty, honesty, and conscientiousness

WHAT THE TEXT OFFERS

Chapters 1 through 3 focus on the self-concept and set the stage for self-understanding and the development of self-esteem. They offer specific activities and suggestions to help the individual develop positive attitudes. Chapters 4 through 6 deal with work adjustment and productivity, the challenges of fitting in and getting along, the development of self-motivation, and cultivation of productive work habits.

Ideas and strategies for developing a good relationship with coworkers and supervisors are presented in Chapters 7 and 8. Chapters 9 through 11 discuss three of the most common problems faced on the job—conflict, stress, and discrimination. Communication is listed by many employers as the number one human relations problem on the job; thus Chapters 12 and 13 are devoted to improvement of communication skills.

Chapter 14 provides specific examples of problems that workers may face as they make day-to-day decisions regarding ethical behavior and standards of conduct in the workplace.

The final chapter prepares the student for the long road to career development. It provides a framework for building a successful, satisfying career in the world of work.

AIDS FOR TEACHING AND LEARNING

As with previous editions of the text, careful attention has been given to writing style and the level of reading difficulty. A survey of teachers and students who used the previous editions revealed that they were easy to understand, especially when compared with books typically used in human relations and business psychology courses at the high school and community college levels. Also, previous users expressed satisfaction and gave high praise about the content of the text. Suggestions regarding additional topics and aids for teaching and learning have been included in this edition.

Some specific features and aids for instructors are:

Objectives. Each chapter begins with a brief outline of expected learning outcomes and achievement expectations for the chapter.

Vignettes. Interesting, realistic cases that illustrate the concepts or ideas to be presented are included in the chapter.

Questions and Projects. Application exercises and activities, at the end of each chapter, are designed to help the learner more clearly understand and *apply* the main ideas presented in the chapter.

Cases. Thought-provoking exercises in decision making and analysis are also found at the end of each chapter.

Teacher's Manual. This manual provides suggested answers to questions and projects and to case problems. Also included are general guidelines for teaching and specific suggestions pertaining to each chapter.

Tests. A variety of questions, in printed form and on disks, may be used for unit testing and for a comprehensive review of student achievement. The answers to the printed tests are given in the *Teacher's Manual.*

Student Workbook. A complete workbook is available to assist students in self-managed reinforcement and additional enrichment activities. Workbook features include self-testing on terms and concepts, programmed reading reviews, practice tests, creative learning experiences for application and reinforcement, and puzzles.

All aspects of the text are based on the premise that the practice of good interpersonal skills is essential if success is to be achieved in the workplace.

Harold R. Wallace
L. Ann Masters

CONTENTS

1

Understanding Your Inner Self

LEARNING OBJECTIVES:

1. Explain the process of personality development.

2. Explain the influence of realistic self-insight on self-esteem.

3. Give examples of personal success in adapting the self-concept as a result of life experiences.

4. Develop supportive relationships with supervisors, coworkers, and personal friends for help in gaining insight and using it to make positive changes in behavior.

Rick felt a hand on his shoulder. He stopped keyboarding and looked at the hand, then up into the face of Ms. Albright, his supervisor. "We need to put those invoices in the mail before the ten o'clock pick-up," she said; "better get a move on." "I'll make it, I'll make it!" Rick responded. There was a little quiver in his voice. "Check with me when you finish. I'll be in the stockroom." At 9:55 Rick proofread the invoice he had just completed, made a final correction, and noted that there were four invoices left in his in-box. "I'll never make it," he whispered to himself. Then he turned off his word processor and stared for a moment at the blank screen. Janet, on

> her way to coffee break, said, "Hey there, dream boy, it's
> your turn to buy the donuts." Rick took a deep breath, said
> "Right on!" and followed Janet into the snack bar.

_____ *To* prepare for your study of the parts of this book that deal with developing your personality, it will be helpful to understand some basic principles. These principles are widely accepted by many highly respected psychologists. Their theories of personality development are based on successful experiences in counseling, teaching, and research. What you will read and what you will experience as you follow the suggestions in the Questions and Projects at the end of each chapter have a solid foundation in the best of modern psychology.

PERSONALITY THEORY

Many psychologists think of the **self** as the center of a person's personality. Your self is what you think of as "I" or "me" deep inside your consciousness. When you really like yourself—when you have a high level of self-respect—you are said to have **self-esteem**. Your self-esteem has many dimensions. Some that are considered important and are sometimes measured with psychological tests[1] are how you feel about yourself in the areas of:

Scholastic ability

Social acceptance

Athletic ability

Physical appearance

Job performance ability

Romantic appeal

Personal conduct and morality

Ability to make friends

---

1. Susan Harter, *Self-Perception Profile for Adolescents* (Denver University, 1987).

ILLUSTRATION 1-1.
How you feel about
your appearance is just
one of the areas to con-
sider when determining
your self-esteem.

You may place a high value or importance on a particular area, such as physical appearance or scholastic ability. If your life experiences contradict how you feel—or how you *want* to feel about your inner self—you can have a serious problem with your self-esteem. How you feel about your inner self— your self-esteem—is always in a state of change and development. How you feel about the importance of the various areas of self-esteem can change, and the influence of your life experiences can shape your self-image or feelings of self-worth. You are in a good state of mental health if the important areas of your self-esteem are evolving to make you stronger, more confident, and better able to succeed in life.

In the next chapter we will discuss some principles of psychology and specific things you can do to achieve success. An important aspect of self-esteem, your **success identity,** will be explained, and you will learn how to develop it. The very important first step toward a success identity is under-standing your inner self and learning how your self-understanding contrib-utes to it. So, now we will explore the basic principles that can help you understand your inner self.

You Are in Control

The first principle of personality theory that you should understand is that *you* are in charge of your life. You can control your behavior by a con-

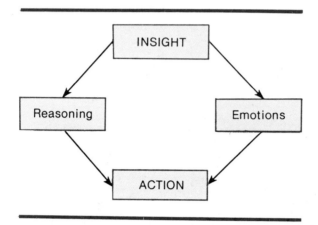

FIGURE 1-1.
The Influence of
Insight on Behavior

scious and thoughtful process. This is true except in severe cases of chronic mental illness. The process of self-control requires **insight** about your inner self. Insight is a clear awareness of your feelings—of what motivates you, what makes you happy, what might cause you to feel anxiety, stress, or depression.

It is not always easy to gain insight about our deepest feelings, motivations, and personality traits. *How* to do this is the next topic. There are benefits of gaining insight about your inner self. You will have a resource of information for logical reasoning, and for exercising your emotional powers, in taking control of your life. That is, you will be able to translate your self-understanding into constructive action—behavior that will build your self-esteem. The following figure shows how insight can influence our actions through our reasoning and our emotions.

Self-Development

Now that we have considered the importance of insight about our inner selves as an essential first step in personality development, we are ready to look at the theory and some basic principles. Most psychologists would agree that self-development is every person's lifetime goal. Carl Rogers uses **self-actualization** as a term for self-development.[2] In one sense it means to bring the inner self in touch with reality—to gain deep insight and self-understanding. It also means that we are always moving toward being the best that we can

---

2. Carl Rogers, *On Becoming a Person* (Boston: Houghton Mifflin Co., 1961).

ILLUSTRATION 1–2.
Self-actualization (self-development) means making the most of our potential for success in life.

be. It means making the most of our potential for success in life. Rogers teaches that we have a natural tendency to strive for self-actualization. But our progress can be seriously delayed or even reversed if we allow what happens in our lives to have a damaging effect on our self-esteem.

The most serious psychological damage you can suffer is the result of closing your eyes (or the eyes of your inner self) to reality. In fact, the symptoms of the most serious kinds of mental illness are losing touch with reality and imagining things that are unreal. Trouble begins when something happens that conflicts with an area of your self-esteem that you feel to be important. It offends your inner self. It is something that you would not expect to happen to someone like you. As a result, a kind of tension—anxiety, distress, or conflict—grows inside you. In very serious cases, you can feel deep resentment and low self-esteem. You may actually hate your inner self.

From a more positive point of view, this theory explains how self-esteem can be improved. If you allow yourself to gain *insight*—to see and understand clearly what is happening in your life—you take the first step in building a positive self-image. You must learn to recognize and accept your experiences as real. Then your **self-concept** (how you see and feel about your inner self) will not be in conflict with your life experiences. You will know and like your inner self. Your tension and inner conflict with reality will disappear. Then the barriers to building your self-esteem will also disappear.

Figure 1-2 shows how the self-concept and a person's life experiences are in agreement when the person is in the process of developing self-esteem—growing toward self-actualization. If you can allow yourself to see clearly and openly all your life experiences as real, the two circles move closer to merge and become as one. Your insight about your inner self agrees with your real-world experiences. You are then able to accept—to truly like—your inner self. When this happens you will experience a high level of self-esteem in all areas that are important to you.

However, if you think that you must deny the reality of many of your experiences, you block out the insights you might gain. Your actions are misdirected because of the unrealistic view you have of your inner self. You will find yourself making excuses or pretending that what happens is unnatural

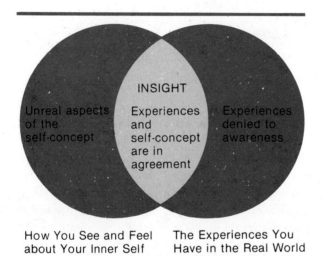

INSIGHT

Unreal aspects of the self-concept

Experiences and self-concept are in agreement

Experiences denied to awareness

| How You See and Feel about Your Inner Self | The Experiences You Have in the Real World | FIGURE 1-2. The Self-Concept |

or unreal. As the circles move farther apart, the area which shows experiences denied to awareness gets larger. Also, the unreal aspects of how you see and feel about your inner self increase. All this creates tension, stress, and anxiety, and prevents self-actualization. Your self-esteem suffers and shrinks.

Here is an example of how this theory of self-development can be applied to a person's life experience. Nan was employed as a hairstylist in a studio which went out of business. In her search for a new job she was offered a position with the Nail Connection. The job was to include nail sculpture, manicures, tip overlays, and similar jobs requiring good eye and hand coordination—**manual dexterity**. Nan accepted the job and went to

ILLUSTRATION 1-3.
A significant other can
be a mentor, friend,
spouse, parent, teacher,
or anyone with whom
you develop a close
relationship.

work with enthusiasm. She assumed that her successful experience in hair-styling was proof of her ability to work successfully at nail sculpting.

But Nan had some problems during her training period. She found that she could not keep up with the other trainees. Also, her instructor gave Nan lower grades on her work. Often she was required to do the work over again. This caused some customers to ask for another technician when they came in a second time. Nan felt crushed. She had expected to succeed in her new job, but she found herself in a struggle to maintain her composure when confronted with what appeared to be failure.

At first Nan made excuses for her inadequate ability to learn her new job. She told her supervisor that she was not feeling well and could not concentrate. She commented that probably the other trainees were more experienced and were faster because of that. But she learned that they were all no more experienced than she was. Another excuse Nan made to herself was that she was not trying hard enough. So she worked as fast as she could, but that seemed to result in more criticism of her work—more failure.

Finally, Nan found herself at a crossroads. If she continued to make excuses and deny the reality of her failure in nail sculpture, she would only create more anxiety and distress for her inner self. It would be very difficult to ignore or hide the reality of her experiences in the training program and, at the same time, maintain her self-esteem in the area of manual dexterity. However, if she accepted her experience as real—as a natural thing to have happen in her life—the result would be different. Nan made the best choice. She confronted the reality of her failure and allowed her inner self to gain insight about this conflict between what she valued and the evidence presented by this experience. She thought, "I tried my best to do the job well and to keep up the pace my supervisor expected. But I was unsuccessful. This experience tells me that my natural ability in the skills required for success in nail sculpting is less than I had thought. But that is all right. I can cope with and accept this failure because there is so much in my life that is rewarding and successful. I do *not* have to be the best at everything. I am good at hairstyling. I have artistic ability and good styling skills, and it is

MASKS: ON OR OFF

Jackie quickly slipped the term paper under her notebook after catching a glimpse of the red "C" on the cover page. She made sure that no one saw the grade as she browsed through the paper in class. She found comments such as "disorganized," "syntax problems," "look up uses of semi-colon," and "do not use jargon." Later, when Jackie and her friend Julie were comparing notes, Jackie said, "He only gave me a 'C' but it really is a good term paper. I think Mr. Nelson gave me a lower grade because something I wrote offended him. He can't stand it when someone comes up with an idea that he disagrees with." There was a pause. Then Julie said, "Do you realize that you just ended a sentence with a preposition?"

realistic for me to have high self-esteem in this occupational area. I need to find a job where I can use my talents." Nan thought about many of her success experiences and felt good. Her experiences in hairstyling were consistent with her self-concept and she was free to grow toward self-actualization.

Do you sometimes wear a mask to hide your real self? If not, you are most unusual. Nearly all of us hide behind a mask sometimes. For example, we may dislike someone, yet we are exceptionally kind to that person to cover up the way we really feel. We may like another person more than we want to show; again, we hide behind a mask of indifference. Of course, if we could not mask our true feelings occasionally, the world would be less civilized. Politeness and good manners are really masks in a way. However, we are not likely to relax and feel good about ourselves if we constantly have to keep up a pretense.

To stay in touch with your inner self requires a similar kind of behavior. As explained earlier, we all need to gain and maintain insight about our inner selves. Also, we sometimes wear masks to avoid direct conflict between the reality of what we experience and how we view ourselves. Here are some suggestions about how to unmask your inner self and make the adjustments to improve your self-esteem.

One effective way to keep in touch with reality and get help you might need to gain self-insight is to develop a close, trusting relationship with someone. Psychologists call this kind of person your **significant other**. In a work situation such a person may be called a **mentor**. Your mentor takes a personal interest in helping you develop and adjust on the job and may help to train you for greater responsibility and future success. Your significant other might also be a friend, spouse, parent, teacher, or anyone with whom you might develop a close relationship. He or she should be someone you can trust enough to share your inner feelings and beliefs about your inner self. With this person you should be able to unmask your inner self and be real—just plain you. You should be able to share anything: your fears, your hopes, your dreams, even your nightmares. With your significant other you should be able to be completely honest in answering questions and in volunteering information about yourself.

This feeling of openness with another person is called the **transparent self**. If you can be transparent with another person, there is an added dividend: *You* discover who you are. In fact, you may not really understand yourself until you have helped someone else to understand you. When you can talk freely and openly with another person you will not feel so alone. You will have a friend with whom you can share the way you are, a friend who will accept you as you are. This kind of mutual trust and concern allows us to see ourselves and understand ourselves. An open and honest relationship will be better able to withstand the upsets that always come along.

Taking off your mask takes courage; it also takes practice. Start now. Find someone with whom you can be your real self. Then you will gradually develop the strength to go without your mask more and more. A life free of self-defeating masks is much happier and more satisfying. If you have an incorrect or distorted self-image because of masks you wear, you may find yourself working hard to live up to the false images and wasting much energy. Put that energy to work finding yourself. The "you" behind that mask is where you must start to build a success-oriented personality.

QUESTIONS AND PROJECTS

1. Think of all the people you know who might be willing and able to talk with you about your emotional problems. Can you identify someone with whom you have a close, trusting relationship—someone with whom you would feel comfortable sharing your innermost feelings?

2. Think of all the people you know who might think of you as a person with whom they could comfortably discuss personal problems. Are you that kind of person? If so, why? If not, why not?

3. We all have mental pictures of ourselves. Sometimes they are good likenesses and sometimes they are not. On a grid like the one shown below, place a check in Column 1 next to the statements that correspond to what you think you are like. In Column 2, on your grid, check the statements you believe other people think you are like. In Column 3, check the statement you would most like to be someday.

a. HOW I FEEL ABOUT MYSELF	1	2	3
Inferior to most of my associates			
Superior to most of my associates			
Self-confident			
Lacking self-confidence			
Proud of my achievements			
Modest about my achievements			
Conceited about my appearance			
Ashamed of my appearance			

b. HOW I FEEL TOWARD OTHERS			
Tolerant			
Intolerant			
Friendly			
Unfriendly			
Like to be with others			

	1	2	3
Dislike to be with others			
Like most people			
Dislike most people			

CASE PROBLEMS

1. Are You a Team Worker?

Maxine has been a brilliant student in high school and college, but she has never shown an interest in school activities. There are two jobs open in the Peerless Bonding Company. One requires that the individual be able to work with others and prefer this type of work to that done alone. The other job is an actuarial job which allows the individual to work alone. When the head of the firm, Mrs. Kenny, interviews Maxine, she suggests that the actuarial job, requiring no group work, might be the better choice for Maxine. This suggestion is agreeable to Maxine, but she wonders how Mrs. Kenny was aware of her preference.

    a.   Do you agree with Mrs. Kenny that participation in school activities indicates a liking for people?

    b.   What jobs can you list that require team effort?

    c.   Which ones can you list that need no ability to work with others?

    d.   Which of your lists is the longer? What does this indicate?

2. Are You Down on Yourself?

Barbara was depressed. It seemed that her work, social life, hobbies, and recreation meant nothing to her. Other people annoyed her more often now than ever before. She found herself lashing out in anger, brooding in frustration, and feeling very "down" most of the time. It seemed she was not really interested in anything or anyone except herself. Barbara began to see her friends slipping away. She began to pick up clues that her employer was not supporting her for a promotion she had been hoping for. Finally, it was obvious to Barbara that she was her own worst enemy. She asked herself, "Is there any way I can turn my life around?"

    a.   Are there any clues in this case that indicate something about Barbara's self-esteem?

    b.   What are the important questions Barbara must answer as she considers how to "turn her life around"?

2

Developing Your Success Identity

LEARNING OBJECTIVES:

1. Develop self-worth by facing reality and behaving responsibly.

2. Use the employment supervisor as a mentor in developing a success identity.

3. Evaluate personal behavior and make positive changes.

4. Explain how to plan to meet personal needs and achieve self-improvement without interfering with or abusing others.

5. Develop the ability to avoid self-punishment and the negative effects of failure when assigned tasks are not carried out satisfactorily.

> *Mary slumped on the couch in her apartment, looked at the ceiling and let the tears flow. "I suppose it's because I'm such a dimwit when math is involved," she mumbled to herself. The papers for her statistics project were scattered on the table and chair where she had been working. "I can't let my friends in the class see how confused and miserable I am when we get together to go over the assignment." Then Greg walked in and said, "Hey, Mary, how are you doing on the statistics project?" There was a pause. "Are you upset or something?" "No," Mary said as she blotted her cheek with a*

tissue. "I just have a headache. The stat's are almost done. But I don't feel like going to that boring review session. Why don't we check the TV schedule and make some popcorn?"

___*It* is not only important to understand yourself, as shown in Chapter 1; you must also feel good about yourself. Confidence and self-esteem can affect your success, and feeling down on yourself can lead to failure. It seems almost inevitable that when you *expect* to fail, you *will*. But when you believe in yourself and expect to succeed, your likelihood of success is greatly improved. You simply try harder when you think of yourself as capable of success. On the other hand, when you fail you betray yourself. You create the image of being a "loser" and this causes others to expect you to fail. Others may actually *encourage* you to fail without wanting or intending to because you seem committed to failure.

YOUR SUCCESS IDENTITY

Have you ever found yourself in a situation like the one Mary is in—feeling like a failure and trying to hide it? Most of us have. Following the guidelines in this chapter can help you to develop your **success identity** and to avoid creating a **failure identity**.

Identity: A Basic Need

Most respected psychologists believe that human behavior is motivated by our striving to meet basic needs. These needs are generally the same for everyone. **Physiological needs**—food, clothing, shelter, freedom from physical pain and danger—are most basic. Satisfying our physiological needs is usually a matter of enjoying what our parents and society provide. After your physiological needs are met, two important **psychological needs** come to your attention. These needs are critical to the development of your self-esteem. We all feel them deeply. They are the need to love and be loved and the need to feel that we are worthwhile to ourselves and others. These two psychological needs are blended together as a single, basic requirement of all mankind—**identity**.

Your unique identity develops in the direction of success or failure depending on how well you meet your needs. As you grow in self-esteem, feeling that you are worthwhile, that you belong and have the love and respect of others, your success identity will grow.

Three Rules in the Game of Life

Now it should be clear that you are in the best of mental health when you are able to fulfill your basic needs by building a success identity—feeling self-worth and feeling that the important people in your life see you as a worthwhile person. It should also be clear that you define for yourself what success means. Your identity—the way you see yourself as a successful person—becomes the focus of your motivation. Your quest to become what you want to become is energized by a vision of your success identity.

There are three guidelines—let's call them rules for living—that must be observed as you build your success identity. They can be summarized in three words: **right, responsibility,** and **reality.**

Right refers to the idea that there are accepted standards that you must follow. You have to know what the people around you expect of you—what is right as they see it. You have to pattern your behavior according to those standards. Successful people can correct themselves when they do things that fall short of the expectations of the important people in their lives. You must develop the ability to evaluate your behavior and to change it when you are wrong. You need to praise yourself when you do what is right. If you fail to correct inappropriate behavior, you will not be able to fulfill your basic need to be worthwhile. You will find yourself moving in the direction of failure—building a failure identity.

© 1987 Kathryn Dudek/
PHOTO NEWS PHOTOGRAPHY

ILLUSTRATION 2–1.
Believe in yourself and expect to succeed; your likelihood of triumph will be greatly improved.

ILLUSTRATION 2-2.
Developing your success
identity on the job begins
with carrying out your
assigned tasks and
responsibilities to their
successful completion.

The President's Committee on Employment of the Handicapped

Responsibility is the ability to satisfy your personal needs without interfering with other people's desires to meet their own needs. You have the responsibility to respect the rights of others. You may not like or agree with everything in your world. It is not necessary to become a robot or a puppet, but if you find that satisfying your own needs creates stress or conflict in your relationships with others, you need to back off. You need to adjust your behavior so that you do not offend or hurt anyone else. You should not use or abuse others in your climb to success.

Reality is the final R. It means that there is a real world. You must understand reality as you strive to build your success identity. The reality of the world is not different for each individual. It is made of hard facts. Hard facts can make the road to success more of a challenge. The theory behind these rules for living is that people who behave inappropriately do so because they have been unable to satisfy their needs. When people fail to satisfy their most basic needs, they will generally lose touch with reality. They are unable to see their world as it really is. In other words, they are unable to get along in life and to behave on the basis of right, responsibility, and reality.

FOUR STEPS TO SUCCESS

Building a success-oriented personality is not an easy task, but making the effort can bring great rewards. You do not develop your personality by picking up a few tricks. To build the desired traits you must *want* to improve; you must *believe* that you *can* improve.

If you are convinced that you should develop your success identity, how should you go about it? Here are four steps in the process of growing toward success:

1. Determine the type of personality you wish to possess. If you analyzed the personalities of those you most admire, you might find a smile; a pleasant and friendly attitude; the use of tact, energy, and motivation; the ability to be calm under stress; skill in conversation; good taste in dress and grooming; or a good sense of humor. Decide to develop within yourself those habits, attitudes, and traits that will best express your ideal personality.

2. Keep in mind the image of the kind of person you wish to become. This mental picture must be so clear and so constantly present that how you behave and conduct your life will bring satisfaction only if it is consistent with your image of the new you. Keep in mind the three R's described above and shape your new image to reflect what is *right*, what is *responsible*, and the hard facts of *reality*.

3. Analyze yourself. Discover and admit to the differences between what you *are* and the ideal image of your new personality. Recognize the traits, habits, and behavior patterns that you need to change. Decide to improve where you need to and to cultivate those qualities that are needed to complete your self-improvement program. You must face the facts squarely and substitute a new strength for any weakness that stands in the way of your reaching your objective.

4. Exercise the traits of the personality you wish to possess. Only by constant attentiveness to your behavior can you be alert to negative actions, and only by practice and effort can you make the desirable traits and habits part of your ideal personality. For example, a genuine liking for people—sincere caring and interest in the lives of others—may be your goal. If you like someone, you want to show it with expressions of approval or small acts of kindness. Ask questions that show you are interested and listen with understanding and a caring attitude. Or suppose you want to build an image of being dependable. Make sure you are always on time for appointments. Put extra effort into completing tasks early if possible, and do the work to demonstrate higher standards than may be required by your supervisor.

ILLUSTRATION 2-3.
Your mentor should
encourage you to
evaluate your behavior.

As you follow these steps in building your success identity, make sure you apply what you learned about yourself through your studying and using the concepts presented in Chapter 1. Recognize that you have special talents and abilities and capitalize on them. What use are your own special gifts and talents if you ignore them? You should make a special effort to build your personality on your good points and cultivate your powers and abilities in areas where you already have a good start.

A MENTOR CAN HELP

A **mentor** is someone who takes a special interest in you and encourages and supports your effort to develop a success identity. An ideal situation is when your employment supervisor accepts the role of mentor. Of course he or she has good reason to help you develop your personality because that will make you a more productive worker. It will also make you more pleasant and easy to get along with on the job.

An important part of mentoring is counseling. You should understand that counseling is a special kind of learning situation. It requires feelings of mutual trust and respect. A warm, understanding person can allow you to be open and honest as you share your feelings and deal with your problems. It is not easy to be open and honest about things that may not be positive.

What you should try to learn from your counselor-mentor ties in with the three R's described in the previous section: what is right, what responsible behavior is, and the hard facts of the real world. In a work situation the process of developing your success identity starts with carrying out your assigned tasks and responsibilities to successful conclusion. This leads to growing feelings of self-worth. Your mentor helps you by being willing to hold you responsible for a course of action even when you might become angry with her or him. If your mentor allowed you to behave in an irresponsible way, you would experience feelings of failure. A popular term for what a caring, firm, consistent counselor-mentor does, is **tough love**. You may have had the experience of having to be tough with someone you care about. This happens when you have to tell a person something she or he may not want to hear, and you experience the discomfort of possibly hurting your good friend. But you take the risk because you care enough about the person, and you know you are helping him or her. If you are so fortunate as to have an employment supervisor or coworkers who will help you with your three R's, and if you have the inner strength to work at learning from them, your success identity will surely grow.

SOME TIPS ON COUNSELING

The person who assists you in your quest of a success identity usually plays the role of counselor. Here is a list of "do's and don'ts" that you and your counselor-mentor should keep in mind. They have been used and found to be effective by professional counselors and therapists.

Focus on Behavior, Not Feelings

You will feel better after you have demonstrated by your behavior that you are a responsible person. You should talk about what you have been doing that makes you feel good or bad. Try to identify self-defeating behavior and correct it. In a way, your behavior can help you understand that you may be your own worst enemy or your own best friend. You cannot expect to change how you feel about yourself without changing your behavior. So you must deal with your feelings by analyzing your behavior.

Focus on the Present

Looking back can be helpful if you need to understand why you feel the way you do about yourself. But dwelling on past failures can be very depressing. You might consider other ways that you might have behaved to lead to a more positive self-image. It is likely that you will know your past failures all too well. But that is only half of the picture. The other half is your strengths—the foundations for future responsible behavior. Think about what you have going for you.

Evaluate Your Behavior

Your mentor should encourage you to evaluate your behavior. This means you will both be making value judgments. When you reach a point where you are able to look at what has happened and what is going on in your life, and realistically evaluate it, you have achieved an important goal along the way to your success identity.

Plan for Improvement

After you have evaluated what you are doing and recognize irresponsible behavior, you are ready to proceed with planning. Your plans should be very specific. They should be designed to lead to improvement. It is very important that you not plan for more than you can realistically accomplish. It is better to move ahead step-by-step, slowly but with the assurance of success.

Make a Commitment

Simply having a plan is not enough. A plan that does not have your firm commitment is likely to fail. Actually, the commitment is to yourself. When the plan is accomplished you will gradually gain a sense of self-worth. It may help to put the plan in writing and to sign a contract.

No Excuses

Of course, not all of your plans will be carried out successfully. When you report that your plan was not carried out or did not work, don't expect your mentor to accept excuses. It will not help to explore at length why the plan failed. The discussion should concentrate on helping you to develop a new plan with a possibly smaller but attainable goal. This may take self-discipline on the part of your mentor because you may not want to discover why your plan failed. You should say to yourself, "I am not interested in why my plan failed. What I need to do is figure out when and how I can accomplish what I want to do."

Eliminate Punishment

Avoiding self-punishment is as important as not making excuses. Reprimands and criticism of your failures will not change your behavior. It will only reinforce your failure identity. Of course you must experience the natural consequences of failure to carry out your plan. However, there is nothing to be gained by inflicting more punishment than that which comes naturally.

This chapter gives you some useful information and a challenge to make the effort and to take the risks to develop your success identity. Accept the challenge and make the effort. You will be rewarded with a measure of personality improvement that can influence your life in a positive way.

Do not expect that success will come quickly and easily; rather, be prepared to build it carefully and slowly. Profit by your unpleasant experiences. Interpret them as opportunities for broadening your outlook and for displaying your own inner powers of resistance, and "keep on keeping on." Believe in yourself, in your ability, and expect success as the final outcome.

QUESTIONS AND PROJECTS

1. One of the hurdles you must conquer in getting a job is talking with an interviewer. How do you rate when you talk with strangers? If you feel insecure in this respect, do some practicing. Talk with someone whom you do not know about employment matters. Possible sources are librarians, teachers in your school whom you do not know, or the placement director in your school. Try to get over your fear before you go to an actual interview.

2. The following test is designed to help you discover your own positive personality qualities. Answer each question with "Yes" or "No."

YES	NO	
_____	_____	If you make a promise, do you always keep it?
_____	_____	If someone, a friend or a coworker, or a member of your family, is in need of help, do you give that help cheerfully?
_____	_____	Are you frequently witty in a sarcastic way?
_____	_____	Do you have a tendency to gain attention by "topping" the remark made by the previous speaker in a conversation?
_____	_____	Are you usually ill at ease with strangers?

		Can you usually avoid being bossy?
_____	_____	Are you critical of others when you feel they are at fault?
_____	_____	Are you able to avoid making fun of other people when they are not present?
_____	_____	Do you frequently laugh at the mistakes of others?
_____	_____	When others make mistakes (in grammar or in pronunciation, for example) do you correct them?
_____	_____	Do you smile easily?
_____	_____	Are you able to praise and compliment other people easily?
_____	_____	Do you frequently try to reform other people?
_____	_____	Are you able to keep your personal troubles to yourself?
_____	_____	Are you suspicious of other people's motives?
_____	_____	Do you frequently borrow the belongings of others?
_____	_____	Do you enjoy gossip?
_____	_____	Are you able to keep out of other people's business most of the time?
_____	_____	Do you avoid talking about yourself and your successes most of the time?
_____	_____	Do you ever use belittling words when referring to those who differ from you in religion, race, politics, or beliefs?

If you are well liked by most of your acquaintances, you will probably answer "Yes" to Questions 1, 2, 7, 11, 12, 14, 18, and 19. Your "No" answers should be to Questions 3, 4, 5, 6, 8, 9, 10, 13, 15, 16, 17, and 20. Give yourself five points for each answer you wrote that corresponds to the instructions given. If your total score is below 70, you need to work on more positive traits.

3. As a new worker you will often find that your work takes longer, and more often fails to meet the quality standards of work done by more experienced workers. How might this affect your success identity? What steps might you follow to soften the effects of these experiences?

4. On a form like the one on the next page, keep an up-to-date list of suggestions you encounter in your work and in your reading that you think might help you to grow. Place a check (✔) beside each suggestion that you try out. If you find the suggestion helpful, put a second check mark beside the first one.

Suggestion	✔	✔

CASE PROBLEMS

1. Bad Start.

On Steffanie's first day of work as a dispatcher for the police department, she arrived thirty minutes late. There had been a power failure at her apartment complex during the night and her alarm clock went off late. She approached her supervisor, Mr. Ryan, to explain what had happened. Before she had a chance to speak, Mr. Ryan told her that Derick, another dispatcher, had to stay an extra half hour to cover for her. He added that if she were late again she would be replaced with someone more dependable. Steffanie had a sinking feeling; and as Mr. Ryan walked away, she knew she had gotten off to a bad start. Later in the day Steffanie made another attempt to talk to Mr. Ryan. She apologized and explained what had happened. This time Mr. Ryan seemed more irritated. He did not look up from his work but said, "Just don't let it happen again. Do you understand?" Steffanie thought to herself that Mr. Ryan's reaction was unreasonable. She began to fear that if she made any mistakes in her work, Mr. Ryan would get angry and fire her on the spot.

    a. Do you agree with Steffanie that Mr. Ryan's reaction was unreasonable? Explain.
    b. How might Steffanie's fears affect her work performance?
    c. What are some ways Steffanie might consider to establish trust with Mr. Ryan?
    d. Do you believe it is important for Steffanie to apologize to Derick? Explain.

2. Private Lives.

Maria Perri has recently been divorced. She feels she is a complete failure. She has returned to work at her old job as an advertising copywriter for Specialty Foods, Inc. Maria is a good worker, but she is not adjusting well after her divorce. She spends a good deal of time talking with others about her unhappy marriage; she cries if reprimanded; and she talks on the telephone for about twenty minutes every day during business hours. Vivian Rugerri has tried to be patient with Maria, knowing her capabilities and realizing the difficulties of her personal life. Now, however, she decides to tell Maria that she must be more businesslike in the office.

a. If you were Vivian Rugerri, what would you say first to Maria?
b. Would you give Maria a warning?
c. Do you think Maria should be discharged?
d. What other action could Vivian Ruggeri take?

3

Developing a Positive Attitude

LEARNING OBJECTIVES:

1. Define attitudes and explain how they develop.

2. Explain how the attitudes of one person can affect the attitudes of coworkers.

3. Explain how a person's attitudes can influence his or her behavior.

4. Explain how behavior creates the image a person presents to others.

"Who does she think she is, Queen of the Universe?" Carl tossed the sweater he had just tried on back on the display table. His friend Bill smiled and said, "Don't let the attitude of that salesperson keep you from buying that sweater. You look good in it." Carl stuffed his hands into his pockets and looked at the floor. Then he slowly began to move toward the door of the sporting goods store. "I don't need the sweater," he said. "When she said that a short guy with a full figure should not wear horizontal stripes—and looked down her nose at me that way, I got her message." "Oh, really?" Carl said, "What was her message?" "That tall, good-looking women think short, chunky guys are dirt."

_____ *An* **attitude** is how a person feels about something. By this definition a major portion of your personality consists of the many different feelings you have. You may like apple pie. You may be attracted to a particular movie star. You may enjoy making pottery or riding a bicycle. At a more intense level, you may fear snakes or crave chocolate shakes.

In another sense, your *attitude* is the general feeling you communicate to others. You will hear someone say, "He has a bad attitude," or, "Her attitude about the project was very positive." Each of us has a unique and complex set of attitudes. They create the general feeling we communicate to those around us. Other terms that are used to describe a person's general attitude are **image** and **aura**. These words suggest that we are constantly sending signals that others pick up. In a way, this actually happens. It is almost as if those around you can "tune in" to your attitudes. Therefore, your attitudes can cause people to be drawn to you and have positive feelings (or attitudes) toward you. Or your attitudes can have the opposite effect, signaling others to avoid you. Your attitudes—or your general attitude—can cause others to see you as attractive or repulsive in varying degrees.

HOW ATTITUDES GROW

It is natural for human beings to be learning constantly. We gain knowledge by studying and by using our logical and critical thinking abilities. We develop skills by practice and careful repetition of behavior with demonstration and coaching to help us improve our abilities. Each kind of learning requires special methods and procedures, and what works for one kind of learning may not work for another. What helps you memorize the anatomy of an insect may not help you learn to swim.

We cannot learn attitudes in the same ways that we develop knowledge or skills. Educators and psychologists who have studied human learning tell us that *emotion* is the critical factor in development of attitudes. Emotions such as fear, joy, anxiety, or compassion seem to shape our feelings about the events in our lives. When an emotion accompanies an event time after time, it creates an attitude or feeling that may be very intense and very difficult to change. Here are two examples to illustrate how your attitudes grow and how they may be changed.

Many of our most enduring attitudes develop when we are very young. As children, most of us have pleasant emotional experiences as we come in contact with soft, fluffy playthings such as stuffed animals or pets. The emotions we feel create positive attitudes toward such objects. However, in an

ILLUSTRATION 3-1. Your attitudes can either cause people to be drawn toward you and have positive feelings, or they can have the opposite effect, signaling others to avoid you.

experiment by psychologists in the 1920's, small children were conditioned to fear and have feelings of rejection toward soft, fluffy objects. The procedure was to allow the child to hold a small pet such as a rabbit, and then ring a very loud bell. The children learned to associate the unpleasant sound and feelings of fear with the animal they were holding. The result was that the children became fearful of any animal or object that brought back the unpleasant memories.

Here is another example of how emotional stress influences attitudes. A large company that was involved in heavy construction found that the frequency of accidental injuries was very high. The training program had stressed safety procedures, and the construction workers were thoroughly acquainted with what they *should* do to protect themselves from injury. The supervisors concluded that while the workers *knew* what they should do, they simply were not doing it. They were found welding without safety glasses. Equipment was being serviced without being turned off (as safety codes required). Power tools were being operated without shields and often workers did not wear gloves when they should have.

One of the supervisors hit upon the idea of having a "debriefing" after each accident. As soon as an accident had happened—preferably when the victim was still experiencing pain and when the blood was still flowing—all work would stop. The accident victim was required to tell other workers what happened, why, and how it might have been prevented. There was a dramatic reduction in accidents under that particular supervisor. When these spur-of-the-moment meetings were held in other construction units, the results were the same—a dramatic reduction in the frequency of accidents. Where lectures on safety practices in training sessions had failed, the emotionally charged learning that occurred in the "debriefing" sessions had a powerful effect on the attitudes of the workers.

These examples show how attitudes are influenced by the intensity and kind of emotion that is present when learning occurs. You will be able to apply this concept later as you develop your own plans and strategies for developing positive attitudes.

YOUR ATTITUDES ARE VISIBLE

Have you ever heard someone say, "Why does she treat me like a baby?" or, "I can read him like a book," or, "Who does he think he is?" or, "She is bluffing."? Remarks like these are clear signals that someone's attitudes are showing. Our feelings and emotions are hard to hide. Of course, you would not *want* to hide a positive attitude. It shines through to create a favorable impression. It is said that "All the world loves a lover." The opposite is also true. We all tend to reject and express hatred toward those we perceive as hateful.

The fact that you see and judge people by their attitudes can be illustrated with this exercise. Think of someone you admire. If you share your ideas about this person with others and have them tell about their favorite people, the illustration will be even more effective. Now, respond to this question about the person you have chosen: What are his or her outstanding qualities? Write these qualities on a sheet of paper. As you review your list, consider how many of the items are *attitudes* that tell something about how the person *feels*, as compared with other qualities such as physical features, what the person owns, or the person's accomplishments. Your list is likely to show two things. First, most of what you consider important in describing someone comes under the *attitude* classification. Second, most of the attitudes are *positive*. Your most admired person's attitudes are visible to you, and it is those attitudes which cause you to admire him or her.

Of course you need to be aware that attitudes are not directly visible. We guess them from evidence we see in a person's behavior. No one can see your inner feelings. But those feelings have such a profound effect on your behavior that you are unable to hide them. Your attitudes are written in your behavior. They give those around you a clear view of what is creating what they see in your behavior.

ILLUSTRATION 3-2.   Look at these four individuals and think about the attitudes each convey. Which of them do you trust the most? To which of them would you go for advice about a serious problem? Which of them would you touch for a small loan?

ATTITUDES ARE INFECTIOUS

It was a busy Friday afternoon in the tire shop. Arnold, Kimberly, and Mark had been installing snow tires for hours, and because of the early snowstorm, customers' cars were lined up in the parking lot. There was not much conversation.

Ray, the shop supervisor, opened the door to the customer waiting area and said, ''Hey, we're behind schedule and it's only an hour 'til we close shop. Can we handle the six cars lined up out there?'' No one said a word. After listening to the clanking of tire irons and the muffled sound of the air compressor for a few seconds, Ray shouted, ''Hey, is anyone alive in this disaster area?'' Kimberly quickly shouted back, ''I am, chief! And I think Mark is showing signs of life. We can handle it!'' ''Great! After work the sodas are on me,'' Ray said as he closed the door. Mark looked up, wiped his forehead, and smiled at Kimberly. ''Sure, I'm alive—and thirsty.'' Finally, Arnold said, ''What a bunch of eager beavers!'' Then he smiled and quickened his pace. By closing time the three were tired but pleased with what they had accomplished.

It seems that how one person feels can have a powerful influence on the others who may be around him or her. This is especially evident when people are involved in a team effort. Yes, attitudes *are* infectious. You have probably experienced the feeling you get when someone like Kimberly in the incident described above causes a positive change in the attitudes of a group. Also, you may recall times when someone had a negative effect by allowing his or her negative attitude to infect others.

YOU CAN CHANGE YOUR ATTITUDES

It may not be easy, but there is one person you can "get tough with" without fear of reprisal. There is, in fact, one person whom you can change. That person is yourself.

Changing your own attitudes can be very satisfying. It can also be enlightening. If you have been having trouble with your supervisor or if you feel you have been criticized too much and too often, you—being human—have probably tried to get even. Perhaps you were sullen. You may have answered abruptly, or you may have threatened to quit. Consider what might have happened if, instead, you said sincerely, "I know I made an error. You are right to tell me about it and I appreciate it. I want to correct the mistake. Is there anything you can suggest or do to help me correct it? I want to improve." No matter how stern and demanding your supervisor may have been, your remarks would probably have created a positive response. Chances are your supervisor would have said, "That's all right. I'm sure you can improve. Here is a suggestion about how to handle it next time."

Developing positive attitudes and eliminating negative ones is the best kind of reforming you can do. But how should you start? There are no rules for self-improvement that will work for everyone. However, the ideas and suggestions on the following pages can be helpful if you have the inner strength to put them to the test. Remember, because attitudes are shaped under the stress of emotions, it may take courage for you to try these suggestions. The reward can be a more positive attitude.

You may feel that you have no need to improve your attitudes—that you already have a positive outlook on life. Perhaps you do; but you will be unique, indeed, if you do not occasionally say something uncomplimentary about a coworker or grumble and complain about something. At a lecture on human relations, the speaker was giving the audience some rules for living. One of the rules was to stop expecting perfection in this world. A member of the audience immediately raised a hand and snapped, "What's wrong with being a perfectionist?" The speaker smiled and answered, "Your tone of voice when you asked that question, for one thing."

Everyone is negative some of the time. Negative feelings, negative attitudes, negative words—all are depressors of the spirit. They all take us—and our hearers—down instead of up. You can get up in the morning feeling great. Yet if you meet four or five friends during the day who tell you of depressing happenings, who complain, or—worst of all—who criticize you and call attention to your mistakes, your happy mood will soon disappear. Fortunately, this works both ways. If you are tired and discouraged, your mood can change when you meet someone who gives you a sincere compliment or greets you with a smile.

We should be climbing toward happiness. At least, we would like to think we could do so. Think of happiness as lying at the top of a long stairway with unhappiness at the bottom. Each negative thought or word takes us one step down. Each positive thought or word takes us one step up.

How can you tell if you need to work on negative habits? Let's try an experiment. Pick a three-hour period when you are usually free to say what you think. From six to nine in the evening is often a time of relative freedom—or from three to six on a Sunday afternoon. Arm yourself with a scratch pad and a pencil. Every time you think or say something negative, write it down. This means *everything*, including, "Is it hot enough for you?" or "You shouldn't wear so much jewelry." Include all the plain, ordinary negative things that we all say and think. At the end of the three-hour period, read them over. You will be surprised, first of all, at the number of items you have written. Then you will wonder when you had time to say or do *anything* positive, which may explain why some of us don't do more things of a positive nature.

Accent the Positive

A negative attitude usually creeps up on us because it is so easy to be negative. It takes no effort to let a feeling of self-pity steal over you. There are disappointments in every day. The easy way is to let them engulf us. It does take effort to replace negative thoughts with positive ones, but the effort is well spent. The way to start is to take the first steps towards being positive:

Smile. If you make yourself turn the corners of your mouth up instead of down, it will be easier to think of something positive to say. Make a real effort to look pleasant and interested in what is going on around you. Under the stimulation of your own interest, those around you may become interesting!

Say Something Pleasant. There are many people in the world who never say anything pleasant. So, for your second step, think of something positive, good-natured, or complimentary to say to someone else at every opportunity. This will do wonders for those around you—and it will also keep you so busy thinking of positive things to say that you won't have time to be negative.

Change Your Negative Statements to Positive Ones. The third step is to change your negative statements in midstream. Say a coworker reaches into the closet and knocks your best coat on the floor. Without thinking, you start to say, "Why can't you watch what you're doing?" But you catch yourself before you get that far. Instead you say, "Why can't—I help you find what you want?" At first you may think of this as being insincere. But keep it up for at least a week. Start a "Let's be more positive" campaign. Watch yourself. When you start to complain about a teacher, an assignment, the weather, or your financial state, stop. See if you can twist that statement around so that it will be positive. You may be surprised at the way your relationships with people improve.

Change a Negative Problem into a Positive Opportunity. After you have practiced on positive statements for a week, you are ready to attack a negative problem. Look around you for some negative situation. Is there a coworker you dislike? Is there a friend who rubs you the wrong way? Whatever it is, try the positive approach. Try to change the situation by being positive.

Let's say you have a friend, Jeff, who gets on your nerves. He talks about himself all the time. He boasts about everything—his car, his job, his school. You think that, without a doubt, he is the most conceited person you have ever met. You may think, "What can I say that is positive that he hasn't already said over and over?" That doesn't matter. Say it anyway. Suppose you meet him at lunch and you don't even have time for a greeting before he begins to tell you about a test on which he knew all the answers. Why not say, "Jeff, I wish I had your confidence." If you keep out the sarcasm and say it sincerely, this may cause Jeff to stop and think a minute. He may not have too much confidence, and his bragging helps boost his self-confidence. He may say, "To tell you the truth, I have always thought you were the confident one." If something like this should happen, the hostility on both sides will begin to evaporate. Now you're probably thinking, "But how do I know this is the way it would go?" No one knows exactly how a conversation will go. It has been proven, however, that this kind of approach results in a positive reply nearly all the time.

Your campaign to become more positive will get you over a big hurdle. When you learn to look at problems with a positive attitude, you can begin to solve them more easily.

USE BEHAVIOR MODIFICATION

A more positive attitude will surely make a difference in your campaign to change yourself. One specific approach to self-improvement that has been successful for many people is to use **behavior modification.** Behavior modification is a procedure for causing behavior change through application of well-known principles of psychology. These principles involve the use of reward and punishment. To use behavior modification to help develop more positive attitudes you need to have your own system of rewards. You may like to work on your car or motorcycle. Or you may prefer to listen to music or sit in a quiet corner and read a favorite book. The thing to do is to think about *you*. What do you like to do best? Take a piece of paper and write down ten to twenty activities that you enjoy. Of course, these activities must be possible in your present circumstances. You can't say you would like to spend a million dollars, because you don't have a million dollars. Just write down the activities you enjoy most, the ones that are possible right now.

When you have your list of rewards drawn up, draw up a contract. Promise yourself that you are going to change in some way. You may decide to study more effectively. You may decide to control your bad temper. Whatever your behavior change is going to be, write it down. Then set up a system of rewards. If you follow your program of change for one hour, you get a certain reward. If you continue for an entire day, you get a better reward, and so on. But remember: the reward is important—just as important as the change in your behavior. If you fail to give yourself a reward, you will stop trying to improve.

You can use a combination of positive attitudes and behavior modification to change others. In a psychology class this theory was tested in the following experiment. One of the students in the class was unpopular. The student was a loner and did not mix with the other students. Two students in the same class wanted to see if they could cause a personality change. They decided to show the first student lots of attention for a few weeks. They talked to their classmate at every opportunity, treating the classmate as they would a popular person. After a few weeks of this attention, a new personality began to appear. The unpopular student actually became popular; talking more freely, laughing with the others, and feeling at ease with the other students. In short, the student became the kind of person the two experimenters had been pretending the student was. Soon, in fact, the original experimenters had a hard time finding their classmate with any free time for them.

The reason for the change in the student's personality was **reinforcement,** a word meaning reward. The student was rewarded for being popular even before becoming popular. The reward worked just as well as it would have if the student had been given a prize for being the most popular person in the class. The results of this experiment show that if we want someone to change, we must make changing worthwhile. If you feel unhappy and someone asks you why you look so sad, you may feel comforted but you are not likely to change. But if someone says, "You look so nice in that blue outfit. It accents your blue eyes," you may find yourself feeling happier.

The rule of reinforcement says that people act in ways that bring some kind of reward. If you want to change your behavior, you must have some payoff, some reward. You will not change if no one notices what you have done. Being ignored is painful. If what you do results in indifference, you stop doing it.

Of all the many factors that influence a person's success, probably the most important is a positive attitude. You can improve your attitude and help others to improve by following the suggestions outlined in this chapter.

Your improvement campaign will pay off in greater satisfaction and in greater ability to fit in and get along on the job and in daily life. The next chapter will provide additional specific suggestions about attitudes you should cultivate.

Chapter 2 described the process by which you can improve your self-esteem and increase your chances for success. Self-esteem works on *you* from within. A positive attitude, as explained in this chapter, works on *others*. As your positive attitude develops, the people around you begin to respond accordingly. They think of you as being enthusiastic, willing to learn, cheerful, and easy to get along with. Their improved image of you causes them to expect positive, productive behavior. As you sense these positive expectations, your motivation to live up to your image is increased. Your self-assurance is increased. The principles of behavior modification begin to work on you. The result is a cycle of reinforcement and improvement, even greater appreciation of your positive attitude, and even higher levels of self-esteem. And, in addition to the beneficial effect of your positive attitude on your own behavior, you find yourself in a new position of power. The influence of your positive attitude on other people allows you to influence *them*. This is particularly true when you apply the principles of behavior modification to change other people in positive ways—to help them improve their self-esteem and positive attitudes.

QUESTIONS AND PROJECTS

1. For one day, casually express appreciation for everything that is done for you. If anyone opens a door, helps you carry anything, passes you the sugar, or is of assistance in any other way, say, ''Thank you,'' and smile. Report to the class whether it made your day any more pleasant.

2. Quick judgments are sometimes made without knowing all of the facts of the case. Make a list of negative statements made to you by others. Opposite the statements, write what you believe may have caused the person to be negative. If possible, learn the *real* reason for each negative statement and compare it against what you *thought* was the reason.

3. Is there somebody that really bothers you—your roommate, a friend, a relative, a coworker? For a change, be positive and don't nag them or complain about it. Instead, see if you can change their behavior. Use the positive reinforcement approach and compliment them for ap-

propriate behavior. While doing this, you must ignore the behavior that annoys you. Use the following plan:

a. Describe in detail the situation you wish to improve.
b. Formulate in detail your plan to increase praise and decrease criticism. Write out some positive statements you might use for example. Using ''P'' as a symbol each time you praise and ''C'' each time you criticize, record your campaign on a calendar for a full week.
c. At the end of the week, report the results. Can you see a change in behavior?

4. Write down five negative statements you have made recently. Can you think of more positive language you might have used? Do you think a more positive approach would have improved the situation? Discuss.

CASE PROBLEMS

1. Criticism Trap.

Sarah Dornbush is a student at the local community college. Only a few of Sarah's former high school friends are attending the college. One of these is Sarah's best friend, Christopher, who is popular with the other students but who seems to take delight in putting Sarah down. Whenever Sarah meets a new friend, Christopher makes some critical remark about the friend to Sarah. Even though Sarah realizes that she should not let Christopher's criticism affect her, Sarah usually breaks off with the new friend. Sarah also notices that she is becoming critical of the other students, especially of their clothes, hair length, and general actions. Sarah seems to be ''catching'' Christopher's negative attitude toward strangers. Suggest a solution to the case from Sarah's point of view.

2. Keeping Distance.

Ken Mears has worked for the ABC Company for five years and has just been promoted to office manager. Jane Harrison has been working in the same office for just two weeks. Her job is in the credit and collections department. Jane and Ken were in high school together. At noon on the first day after Ken has accepted his new job, Jane asks Ken to go to lunch as her guest to celebrate the promotion.

a. If you were Ken, what would you say to Jane?
b. What would be the best attitude for Jane to assume toward Ken in the future?

    c. What would be the effect on the office force if Ken were to accept?

    d. What attitude should Ken have toward all his former coworkers—and Jane?

4

Fitting In and Getting Along

LEARNING OBJECTIVES:

1. Explain the employer's view of fitting in and getting along.

2. Describe how to be tactful in a variety of situations.

3. Develop a cheerful disposition and sense of humor.

4. Understand and cultivate humility, and avoid conceit.

5. Avoid self-pity, grumbling, and resentment.

6. Recognize and work to overcome objectionable habits.

7. Develop a caring and sharing attitude.

8. Develop a desire for self-improvement.

Will Rogers was famous for saying that he never met a person he did not like. But most of us are not so forgiving and tolerant of personality defects in others. Consider the situation Cynthia found herself in. She had a B-plus average in her courses as a student in electronics at the community college. But after six months on her first job in television repair, Cynthia was dismissed. Her record of performance ratings indicated that she had always done her assigned work exceptionally

> *well. Why did Cynthia lose this job? Some of the last entries in her personnel file were: "Does not respond well to constructive criticism." "Seems to annoy fellow workers." "Emotionally immature." "Would rather argue than listen." Is Cynthia's case unusual? How might she have avoided this crisis in her career?*

___*When* employers are asked to give the most frequent causes of failure on the job their answers fall into a familiar pattern. Almost always the reasons relate to failure to fit in and get along with others. You might expect that people most often fail because they lack the critical job skills and ability to perform required tasks, but this is simply not so. Many research studies have documented this fact. Your employer is more likely to tolerate inadequate job performance than to allow you to continue working when you are a source of interpersonal conflict.

In Chapter 3 you were encouraged to develop a self-improvement plan— a plan for eliminating negative attitudes and creating a positive attitude. This chapter can provide you with some specific ideas to include in your plan. You should now be prepared to assess your own personality and find out what you need to do to improve and prepare for successful employment. Success-related personality factors can be identified because there has been so much research on the subject. The results of this research consistently point out a number of common personality factors as important. This chapter highlights those traits that are most important in helping a person to fit in and get along on the job. Those factors most critical for being productive and learning to do the job well are discussed in Chapter 5.

You do not have to be the most popular, interesting, or entertaining person in the crowd. You will fit in and get along with your coworkers and supervisors if you cultivate a few positive characteristics that nearly everyone expects and appreciates. The way you get along with your coworkers will have much to do with your job success and promotional chances.

LEARN TO BE TACTFUL

According to Webster's dictionary, **tact** is "a keen sense of what to do or say in order to maintain good relations with others without offense." It is

ILLUSTRATION 4-1.
If you are tactful, you will make life infinitely easier for yourself and those around you.

a sixth sense that makes us aware of what would be fitting to do or say at a given moment. It puts us in the other person's shoes. If you are tactful, you will make life much easier for yourself and those around you. Tact involves understanding the other person's needs and wishes.

Simply wanting and intending to be tactful is not good enough. It takes good judgment and sometimes careful wording of your remarks. Consider each of the following situations and describe how you might be tactful if faced with the problems that may arise.

Dismissing unwanted callers

Making visitors or customers feel at ease if they are kept waiting

Avoiding answering confidential questions that outsiders ask about the business

Ascertaining a caller's business before disturbing your supervisor

Giving callers the impression that, no matter how trifling the reason may be, your supervisor will be glad to see them if possible

Suggesting changes or improvements without giving the impression that you are critical of the way things are

Asking for a promotion or raise

Responding pleasantly and courteously when you have been spoken to in a rude manner

Offering suggestions to other people in such a way that their feelings will not be hurt unduly

Helping to settle differences between two fellow workers without appearing to take sides

Expressing an opinion that is different from that of another person without being disagreeable

Asking the name of someone whose name you have forgotten

Sending a sales representative away satisfied with the interview, though no sale was made

Asking a customer to pay a past due account

Explaining to a customer that store policy does allow for an article to be returned

BE CHEERFUL

No single trait will endear you to your coworkers and your supervisors as will the ability to look on the bright side, to deal with others with a light

ILLUSTRATION 4–2. Like cheerfulness, a sense of humor is something almost everyone appreciates.

touch. Cheerfulness is a virtue, even though we seldom hear anyone preach about it. It is one that makes working well with others remarkably simple. Don't take things too hard, keep a light touch, and your work with others will be smooth and successful.

Actually, cheerfulness is the result of being able to accept yourself and to accept others. When you can take off your mask and be your own self, you will have no need for the defenses you have built up to hide your real self from the world. When you accept yourself, you also discover that most of your troubles happen because of what you do. You take things hard when you are concerned too much with yourself.

When you can change, when you can become more cheerful, you will be able to think of other people more, and less of your own shortcomings. Cultivate the light touch; learn to be cheerful. It only takes practice.

DEVELOP YOUR SENSE OF HUMOR

Like cheerfulness, a sense of humor is something almost everyone appreciates. There are two typical reasons why some people appear to have no sense of humor. First, they may not appreciate humor most of the time. What appears to be funny to others is not funny to them. The second reason is that the person *underreacts*. When others are breaking up with laughter, this kind of person barely cracks a smile. Such a person may actually enjoy a very funny joke but does not express the enjoyment in visible action.

You may have either or both of these problems with your sense of humor. The second problem is a bit easier to deal with. If you sense that you are underreacting to humor, you should make an effort to be more expressive. It may make you feel a bit uncomfortable to laugh out loud when you normally only smile or giggle. But you can bring your reactions up to the level with which others feel comfortable. A good rule of thumb is to observe the typical reactions of others. Of course, you should not pattern your behavior after someone who tends to overreact to humor. Being too loud or carrying on too enthusiastically can be worse than underreacting. But you should *use* your sense of humor and good judgment to adjust your responses to humor so that others will recognize and appreciate your sense of humor.

If you find that others see humor where you do not, you have a more serious problem. You will need to cultivate your sense of humor. If, when others see humor in a situation and you do not, you may be acting as if you "get it" when you do not. Under those circumstances, you very likely might make a fool of yourself. It is better not to pretend. If you are not responding to humor, you may appear to be insensitive, bored, or indifferent. In fact, you may give the appearance of being a snob.

Here are a few suggestions about how to cultivate your sense of humor.

1. Have a friend help you by discussing what he or she sees in comic strips, jokes in magazines, and commentaries written by people who are famous for their wit.

2. Study literature such as Shakespeare's play *Taming of the Shrew.* and Robert Service's poem *The Cremation of Sam McGee.* Look for similar situations in your social life and at work. This is a way to find and sense humor in your everyday life.

3. After watching a comical television program, movie, or play with friends, discuss the humorous highlights with them. This will help you discover and be more sensitive to humor. But be sure not to ruin the performance for them by asking questions when they are involved in listening and watching.

4. Look for the humorous side to mishaps and problems you may have. There are many examples in history and literature showing how people can face misfortune and adversity with a sense of humor. Of course, there is a fine line between enjoying the humorous side of an event and degrading or making fun of someone. You should not allow a joke on yourself or someone else to be a put-down.

CULTIVATE HUMILITY

We have discussed the importance of self-esteem in earlier chapters. Also, we have suggested that you should not mask your real feelings—that you should be open. Now it is important for us to consider what may seem to be the opposite of self-esteem—**humility.** Actually, the truly humble person has a clear, accurate self-image, appreciates his or her good qualities, and is able to communicate self-worth openly. It is **pride** that is the opposite of humility.

It seems that it is human nature to admire humility in a person and to show disdain for pride. Here we are not referring to the kind of pride associated with patriotism or loyalty. We mean the kind of pride that is demonstrated by bragging, by showing off, and by creating a false impression of superiority. Another word for this kind of pride is *conceit.*

To cultivate humility you should first be aware of what you may be doing to create the wrong impression. You may find yourself not listening when someone else is talking about herself or himself. Instead you are thinking of what *you* are going to say. You may be searching for a way to "get one up" on the other person. If the person is talking about a new motorcycle, you point out that you own one that is newer, faster, or better in some way. If he or she had an accident that needed ten stitches in the emergency room, you tell about how you had twenty stitches when you had *your* accident. If you can catch yourself and avoid talking about your experiences in a way that makes you look better than others, you will be demonstrating humility.

Another approach to developing a humble attitude is to analyze yourself, identifying ways that you are special. Also identify ways that you are *not* so special—not superior to others. If you are honest with yourself, you will likely come to the conclusion that while you have good reason for self-esteem, you are not superior to others. You have no good reasons to brag, to show disdain for the accomplishments of others, or to be conceited. You should learn humility by *being* humble—not by trying to *act* humble. A mask of humility is transparent. Sincere humility shows through in your personality if you follow the suggestions outlined above to avoid creating the wrong impression.

AVOID SELF-PITY

A conceited person talks about himself or herself to create an impression of superiority. Another habit that can irritate other people is self-pity. You may talk about your personal problems until others get tired of hearing about them. Even if you do not say anything to others, simply dwelling on your own problems can drag you down. If you have this habit, you should wipe out once and for all the "poor little me" feeling. Self-pitying thoughts will creep into our minds unless we are on guard. There is too much self-pity in the world, and it is followed by an even more destructive attitude—resentment.

OVERCOME GRUMBLING AND RESENTMENT

"That woman is a—" "Hold it!" Fred interrupted, "You don't want to say something like that about someone you have to work with every day." "I know," Janice said with a sigh. "She just gets on my nerves. Always grumbling and complaining about something, never saying anything positive.

> I agree with some of her complaints, but she just goes on and on." "I know," Fred responded, "But you can tell she is preoccupied with all the bad things in her life. I have to work with her, too. But I avoid her the rest of the time."

Resentment, when people express it openly, comes out as grumbling and complaining. Too much of this kind of conversation depresses friends and coworkers, even if there are good reasons for it. Eventually, the grumbler finds himself or herself shut out and alone. Nothing is so destructive to the personality as is resentment.

One way to cure resentment is by acting. Don't just sit there and brood. Do something! Any kind of positive action will help eliminate resentment, but the best cure is action that you enjoy. Perhaps you have done poorly on a test and you deeply resent the person who got the top grade. Thinking about your resentment—nursing it to keep it warm—will not help. Nor will additional study be effective while you are in a resentful mood. Instead, do something you enjoy that is active. Play tennis, join a square dance group,

Richard Younker

ILLUSTRATION 4–3. Combining action with enjoyment will overcome any resentment and put the original cause for resentment in proper perspective.

swim, go for a ride, do anything that is fun for you. Combining action with enjoyment will overcome any resentment and put the original cause for resentment in proper perspective.

OVERCOME OBJECTIONAL HABITS

Just as there are habits and techniques you should cultivate for success in the world of work, so there are habits that you should avoid. Unfortunately, we never notice most of these unwelcome habits. You may notice them in others but fail to recognize that you may be guilty, too.

Most of the following objectionable habits come under the heading of bad manners. You may not realize that you have some bad habits, but certainly you should make an effort to correct any faults once they have been called to your attention. Ask a close friend to check you against the following list—and you do the same for your friend. Then make a sincere effort to eliminate any that you do—even occasionally.

Drumming or tapping with fingers, toes, or a pencil

Humming or whistling under your breath

Sniffling

Clearing your throat

Sucking your teeth

Coughing or sneezing without turning your face and covering your mouth with a handkerchief

Fussing with your hair

Playing with rings, beads, or other jewelry

Adjusting your collar, cuffs, or belt

Scratching your head

Chewing gum

Yawning

Backslapping

Whispering when others are speaking

Wrinkling your brows

Slamming doors

Banging telephone receivers

Dashing in and out of rooms

When you know which of the objectionable habits are to be eliminated from your habit structure, start on just one at first. When it is eliminated, go on to the second. To eliminate an undesirable habit, be conscious that you possess it; honestly desire to get rid of it; and stop it *now*.

WANT TO GROW AND IMPROVE

A number of studies have been made of successful young people. One such study asked many questions concerning factors that may have influenced their success. In their answers, successful beginning workers said they did not expect success to come without effort. They stated that nothing comes to those who only wait for it. They believed that successful people must work hard, adjust to life's problems, want to improve, and make a determined effort to become more capable.

The desire for improvement is a wish to enhance oneself in value or quality. Everyone has vague desires of improvement. With success, however, you become aware of what is involved in achieving greater success and are able to set more realistic goals. For example, the untried student may dream of handling scores of workers with a word. A businessperson who knows what is involved in leading others and who knows the difficulties likely to be encountered will set goals within the realm of possibility. For this very reason, a realistic desire for improvement is usually stronger after the worker has had some success in work.

You probably know people who are bitter because they have not succeeded even though they have done everything they have been told to do. Unfortunately, doing only what you are told to do or meeting the minimum expectations of a job is not enough to bring success.

To be a successful worker you must go beyond the call of duty. You must do what is expected of you—plus. In adding this extra quality that is needed for success, you must not be aggressive or rude. Instead, you should, in a quiet and confident way, give more thought and work to the assignment. This plus quality has two parts. One part is a desire for improvement; the other is doing something about the wish to improve.

The desire for improvement may be expressed in being proud of the growth of your firm, in watching and helping that growth. If you have this pride, you will also be proud of the amount of work you can do in a certain time. One of the joys of any kind of work is pride in good work. Even after the day's work is finished, you can express pride in your work. Read the newspapers and magazines for items that may affect your firm. Keep in touch with current and local affairs.

The companies for which you will want to work will be sure to appreciate the ability to share. All businesses are working hard to create goodwill with their customers and their potential customers. If the employees of a firm possess the same quality, it will help the firm create a good feeling with the public. Sometimes it may appear that selfishness is rewarded and unselfishness unnoticed. Such instances do occur, of course, both in the employment community and in all other areas of living. However, the results of an unselfish attitude toward others will be evident in your personality, if you continue this trait. Appreciation of unselfishness may be slow, but it will be sure.

If you have the opportunity, talk with experienced businesspeople about selfishness and unselfishness in business. You will discover that most people have a basic respect for fair play and unselfishness. Your coworkers will dislike you if you violate these basic values. To be accused of unfairness or selfishness would cost you more than anything you might gain by being unfair or selfish.

You may express unselfishness by lending or sharing your materials and equipment with other employees where there is a need. You will give information, time, or services when your department is working under pressure. You will work overtime when this is necessary to complete the job on time. When there are unpleasant duties to be done, you will do your share willingly.

All of these suggestions are familiar to you. Most of us have grown up with such maxims. All that is necessary is to make them habitual actions.

LEARN TO SHARE THE GLORY

There is another side of unselfishness that is not often stressed, yet it is even more important to the smooth working of a business team. This is the ability to accept gracefully that your superior will often be praised for your work, ideas, or the plans. Developing this kind of unselfishness is not easy. In our fiercely competitive society, most of us try to shine individually. We dislike sharing with others honors rightfully belonging to us. Yet an old saying is true: You can get anything done so long as you don't care who gets the credit.

There are steps in developing this cooperative kind of unselfishness. First, refrain from talking about your high skills, high grades, and successes in general. Rather, help another person to accomplish something and then praise the one you helped. This is the way to begin. After a while you will receive a greater feeling of pleasure from the success of the one you helped than you ever would from your own successes.

From this beginning it is a short step to a glow of pride when others in your department or your company achieve honors in which you had no share. Envy and jealousy—two most unattractive traits—can be eliminated from your nature with this sort of practice. All it takes is practice each day. If you can become the kind of person who is pleased when you hear words of praise for someone else, you will have taken a giant step toward emotional health.

DESIRE FOR CIVIC SHARING

As you grow in your ability to share with your fellow workers, you will need to expand your horizons to the community in which you live and work. You will then have civic or social consciousness—you will want to further existing institutions if they are working for the public good. If you see a

ILLUSTRATION 4-4.   Working for public betterment is one of the hallmarks of an adult person.

need for change in the local government bodies, you will be willing to do your share to bring such change about. Working for public betterment is one of the hallmarks of an adult. You know, of course, that business depends on society and that society regulates business. You know, too, that the services of all legitimate institutions have value. You also serve society in your capacity of employee, no matter how humble your position.

When you are called upon to contribute to your United Fund, the Red Cross, and the various other drives, you are glad to do so. The request usually comes through the business that employs you, and that business is judged by the social consciousness of its employees. If you are asked to work for some civic organization for the general good of the community, you are glad to be of help. When requests for information come to you, you answer them promptly and courteously. You obey the laws of your community; you set a good example to others in your conduct and in your speech.

As you mature as a worker, you in turn become a leading citizen of the community—one to whom your fellow citizens will turn for leadership. This day will come more quickly if you get the feeling of civic responsibility early— responsibility for those less fortunate than you, responsibility for helping to maintain and carry on the worthwhile institutions of today. Your service to society is a debt you owe in payment for the privileges that are yours.

QUESTIONS AND PROJECTS

1. By what outward signs do you judge people when you first meet them?

2. Practice being cheerful until cheerfulness becomes a fixed part of your personality. Act and look cheerful, no matter how you feel. Stand up straight; smile at everyone; look like the world is yours. Try this exercise for one week and report the results.

3. How do you think an employer would estimate you on the following lists of traits, and on what outward evidence would an employer base an opinion?

ARE YOU	OR ARE YOU
persistent	a quitter
sociable	unsociable
careful	careless
accurate	inaccurate

industrious . . . . lazy

enthusiastic . . . . indifferent

self-confident . . . . self-conscious

ambitious . . . . satisfied to ''get by''

punctual . . . . tardy

agreeable . . . . disagreeable

optimistic . . . . pessimistic

patient . . . . impatient

thrifty . . . . spendthrift

modest . . . . vain

4. The way to avoid arguments is to *relax* and wait for the whole story. The next time you are tempted to argue with someone, say nothing. Just wait and listen. Write down the result of your experience. Did you accomplish anything? Do you feel this is a helpful solution for you?

CASE PROBLEMS

1. Your Best Friend Won't Tell You.

Peggy works in a word processing unit. One day four of the other employees whose desks were near Peggy's made an appointment to talk with the supervisor, Mrs. Washington. When the meeting was held, Peggy's coworkers told the supervisor they would all like to have their desks moved away from Peggy. When asked their reasons, they said they couldn't stand Peggy's disagreeable body odor. Mrs. Washington thanked them and promised to do something about the problem.

    a. Assuming you are the supervisor, how would you handle this problem?
       1. Would you tell Peggy that her coworkers had complained? Why or why not?
       2. Would you begin your conversation with Peggy with a question or with a statement?

    b. Discuss the matter with four of your classmates. After you have agreed on a solution, write the exact words you think you would say to Peggy.

    c. As an alternative to writing the supervisor's conversation with Peggy, perform your version of the solution to this problem as a role-playing assignment.

2. Getting the Lowdown.

Joe Garcia has just started in his first job as a salesperson in the home furnishings section of a large department store. One of the older employees, Mr. Parker, asks Joe to lunch at the end of his first week in his new job. During lunch, Mr. Parker talks freely and critically about the head of the department, the management policies of the store, and how hard it is to inject any new ideas. Joe agrees, adding that he has found it rather hard to work with Miss Green, the head of the department. "She seems to know all the answers," Joe says, "and doesn't respect the ideas of others. I guess she's afraid they might be better than her own."

The next day Joe is called to the general manager's office and berated for criticizing the department manager. Joe immediately realizes that his luncheon companion has reported Joe's comments. He is very angry and decides to be less friendly with the older employees in the future.

a. What do you think of Joe's solution to the problem? Can you suggest another solution that might be more effective?

b. What should a new employee's attitude be toward early friendship with other employees?

c. If you had been Joe, how would you have answered Mr. Parker when he criticized the policies and management of the store? Why?

5

Developing Your Productivity: Motivation

LEARNING OBJECTIVES:

1. Explain the meaning and importance of enthusiasm.

2. Develop a commitment to avoid tardiness and absenteeism.

3. Develop the ability to show initiative and be resourceful.

4. Explain the meaning and importance of going the extra mile.

5. Develop skills in self-initiated learning.

Mildred and Phil, two fast-food restaurant managers, were sharing a ride home after work. "The bad news for me today was that I had to let one of my best people go," said Phil. "But why would you do that?" Mildred asked. Phil replied, "She just wasn't dependable. When she was on the job she was topnotch. But you can't run a business when you don't know whether or not your people are going to show up." Why do you suppose Phil was so concerned about dependability that he was willing to fire a competent employee and replace her with one less capable?

_In_ Chapter 4 we focused on attitudes that are most important to help you fit in and get along with others in your employment situation. Here the focus is on attitudes and habits that can increase your productivity. They will help you get the job done. In addition to developing a pleasant personality, you will be learning to become a good worker.

CONCENTRATE ON YOUR JOB

A good work attitude includes **enthusiasm,** both for the work and for the firm that employs you. Enthusiasm is not a single trait. Rather, it is positive energy expressed in many of your personality traits. When you are enthusiastic you may seem to bubble with energy. Your positive energy seems to spread among other workers, and that "down-in-the-dumps" feeling disappears. Enthusiasm accounts for a major share of what creates success on the job.

Dependability

If someone says you are dependable, what does it mean? In most cases, it means you do what you say you will do. It sounds quite simple, doesn't it? Yet workers with the best of intentions are often labeled as undependable. They hate to hurt another person's feelings by saying no. They say they will get the report out by five o'clock, but they really know they won't be able to do it. Dependable people, however, do not say yes unless they are certain they can carry out their promises. In effect, when you say you will do something you create a contract. A written contract might seem more important to you, but a spoken promise is just as important. If you are a dependable worker, you will do your work well. You will not be an alibi artist. If you make a mistake, you will admit it and suggest a way of correcting it.

Being dependable also means that you will be at work when you are expected. You will be on time, and you will use your time well. You should realize how important it is for an employer to be able to count on having all employees at work when they are supposed to be there. Even worse than workers failing to show up for work is failing to show up without giving any warning ahead of time.

Consider what happened to Neil. He worked as a dishwasher in a restaurant about five miles from his home. On the way to work on his bicycle, Neil had a flat tire, which took nearly an hour to repair. While he was at the service station fixing the tire he _could have_ telephoned to let his supervisor know he would be late. But he was somewhat shy, and the prospect of ex-

ILLUSTRATION 5-1.
Being dependable means
that you arrive to work
on schedule, and you
use your time well.

plaining his problem over the phone made him feel uncomfortable. So Neil
was nearly an hour late as he approached his place of employment. Now the
anxiety he felt about facing his employer was even greater. Not having the
courage to go to work late, Neil did not show up at all. To make things
worse, he did not call to explain his absence. The next day Neil's worst fears
were realized. When he arrived at work his supervisor had a pink slip waiting. Neil lost his job because he was not dependable.

Was the supervisor's reaction too severe? Perhaps so. However, one of
Neil's problems was not appreciating how his supervisor would feel about an
expected tardiness or absence. When you understand the problems this
can cause on the job, you may not think the supervisor's action was
unreasonable.

You would very likely consider taking money from the cash register as
dishonesty, something you would never do. Yet failure to come to work, tardiness in coming to work, and tardiness in returning from lunch periods
and coffee breaks are just as serious, just as dishonest, as taking money from
the cash drawer. You can control your attendance and punctuality. You
may doubt your skill, your manners, or your appearance, but you need not

doubt your ability to get to work every day a few minutes before your work day begins. Attendance and punctuality form an important block in building your success. Don't let this block crumble. Be there—and be on time.

Use Your Time Well

When you work, you are paid for your time and the way you spend it. In business, time is money; many of the good work habits you will need involve the proper use of time. For example, you will arrive at work on time— or even a few minutes early—every day. The importance of habit cannot be stressed too much. It shows others that you value your job, but the greatest value in arriving on time is its effect on you. This is best illustrated by what happens when you are late for work. Everything you do becomes shaded by the fact that you were late. You are behind with your work, so you hurry to catch up; because you hurry, you make mistakes; making mistakes causes you to become flustered, so you hurry faster. This circle of hurry and errors goes on all day. On the other hand, if you come to work early, you are relaxed when you start your first task. Relaxation helps you work rapidly and accurately. Working in this way brings you a feeling of satisfaction, and this feeling helps you with the next task at hand. The result is a circle of excellence that works for you all day.

Leaving early should be avoided. Clock watchers seldom get promoted. You are using time that belongs to the company if you leave early for or return late from lunch and coffee breaks, or if you spend extra time talking in the washroom. Time is involved in the rules that govern your work. Whatever the rule may be, you must abide by and not exploit the rule.

DEVELOP YOUR SELF-MOTIVATION

Jerry was a student in a high school cooperative education program. The telephone rang in the office of her teacher-coordinator, Luis Perez. "This is George Nelson, Jerry's training sponsor. Can we talk about a problem we're having with Jerry?" "Of course," Luis said. "What's going on?" "Well, as you know, in this kind of business we can't always hover over our people and tell them every little thing to do. But when Jerry comes to a slack period, or when she completes an assigned job, she disappears. Usually I find her in the coffee room or out having

a smoke." "I understand," Luis said. "We'll have a talk."
Later, in discussing the matter with her teacher, Jerry said,
"But Mr. Perez, I always do what I'm told, and they tell me I
do good work. What do they expect?"

What is **self-motivation?** Is it busy work? Or is it rather a drive within yourself to get things done? How can you acquire this drive if you do not possess it now? As your needs change, the spark that motivates you will change also. Right now, you may be working for grades—a passing grade or a high one. Or you may be interested in the approval of someone whose opinion is important to you. These motivating influences are what we call external or extrinsic ones. This means that the spur to achieve comes from the outside. In time, this external motivation may be partly replaced by internal motivation. Internal motivation is the kind that comes from within, such as the satisfaction that comes from doing a good job.

World Bank Photo by James Pickerell

ILLUSTRATION 5-2.
Internal motivation is
the kind that comes
from within, such as the
satisfaction that comes
from doing a good job.

We all use some of the common ways to put off applying self-control. We get a drink of water; we adjust the ventilation; we become distracted at the slightest interruption and find it hard to pick up where we left off. All of these preparations for work must be forgotten. The best way to begin working is simply to begin. Get started with a stubby pencil. Save that drink of water for a reward at the end of your first completed page. Adjust the ventilation as a reward for the completion of your second. If you use self-control the first few times, you will form the habit of concentrated effort. With this habit, you will find yourself becoming a much more productive worker.

There is no simple formula for controlling efforts and emotions. By trial and error you will discover ways that work for you. Just remember that practice in self-control builds strength. The following list will provide you with suggestions for developing self-motivation. If you find abilities in this list that you would like to acquire, begin now to try to make them a part of your personality.

Ability to work at a task that does not appear to offer immediate interest or pleasure

Ability to work instead of participating in pleasant sports or entertainment when the work cannot be postponed

Ability to begin a necessary task without waiting until the last minute

Ability to work in the presence of distracting influences—physical discomfort, noise, emotional stress, heat, etc.

Ability to work when weary, even late at night if the occasion demands "burning the midnight oil"

If you have never worked or if you have never put in a full day's work for a day's pay, you will have little conception of what this means. Any job contains a certain amount of routine work, and most of this work is concentrated in the beginning levels. The way to emerge the victor over drudgery is to make your habits work for you. Work habits, like other habits, are built up day by day. It will pay you to form good work habits from the very beginning of your first job.

Taking Initiative and Being Resourceful

Initiative means the energy or ability displayed in an action that opens up new areas. To have initiative means to have self-reliance, originality, enterprise, and resourcefulness. You can hardly read such a definition without thinking of the selling field. The successful salesperson *must* have initiative. As a salesperson you must think of new methods of reaching your customers; you must sometimes seek out new customers; you must stress the new features of your merchandise. Initiative is a central trait in selling, but it is useful in all jobs. When you are beginning in many occupations, you may not find many important situations calling for the use of initiative. The first job calls for following orders implicitly, doing what you are told to do without question. In time, though, you will grow through experience and practice. You will then be given larger responsibilities and demands that call for independent thinking and action.

When to use initiative, as well as how much to use, calls for the use of your own good judgment. Again, put yourself in your employer's place. How would you like your employee to proceed? The new salesperson should not rearrange displays so they will look more attractive. This may be viewed by some supervisors as showing too much initiative. On the other hand, failure to act in a crisis when there appear to be no predetermined rules may be even worse. For instance, suppose a customer is upset upon receiving merchandise other than that ordered. As a salesperson, you should certainly show your concern. You should say that something will be done about the situation—whether you had been previously instructed to do so or not.

ILLUSTRATION 5–3.   You show initiative when you learn all you can about the business and your place in it.

As a newcomer in the businessworld, you may find it hard to know just how far you should go in the matter of doing things on your own. Sometimes the rules of the organization make it necessary to follow a set pattern in everything that is done. In most cases, however, the follow-the-rules phase lasts only a short time. Before long you will be faced with an emergency. The executive who is to sign all orders may be in the hospital or out of town. When something of this nature happens, the only thing you can do is weigh the matter carefully. What would be the results if you followed the rules? Would you lose an order? Would you cause a visiting executive to take the wrong plane? If the consequences of following the rules are worse, in your judgment, than acting on your own, you must have enough initiative to act on your own. The only requirement is that you think the situation through carefully and make your decision on the basis of facts and objectives and not on panic.

Resourcefulness is a help at any level of business. If you can make do with whatever is at hand, you are being resourceful. You are resourceful if you can imagine the possible consequences of two actions and choose the one more likely to meet with success. The motto THINK will help you be more resourceful.

Be willing to work. Although it may seem obvious to explain that a worker must be willing to work, many workers seem to spend their time in other ways. There are a number of clues which tell your supervisor or employer how willing a worker you are. You willingly perform the task that is assigned to you. After the assignment has been made, you arrange your duties so that the work is completed on time. Because mistakes can be serious, you take great pains to be accurate. You take pride in your work.

Go the Extra Mile

How do you know if you can go the extra mile? One clue is this: Can you keep going when the going gets rough? Another clue is whether you can stand on your own two feet. People who lean on others, who always ask for help, or who are filled with self-pity, are not the kind who go the extra mile. They are the ones who give up. All people have problems, but those who can go the extra mile master their problems.

It takes courage to go the extra mile. It also takes courage to admit your mistakes. Once having admitted them, you will find your path much smoother. If you cover up your mistakes, you will spend far too much time making excuses, blaming your troubles on others, and depending on the alibi. If you admit an error in judgment, you may feel ashamed—or you may even be punished—but eventually you will be respected for your honest admission.

You demonstrate your ability to go the extra mile by taking responsibility for your errors, by facing irritations without reacting to them, by defending the policies of the firm, by ignoring pettiness and gossip that may involve you, by standing up to be counted for that which you know is right. You go the extra mile when you cheerfully perform the difficult, tedious, or unpleasant task when it falls to you. You go the extra mile when you perform your work with poise, dignity, and patience although conditions at work or in your private life may be distressing. You go the extra mile when you do not take unnecessary advantage of illness, physical handicaps, or interruptions to avoid work.

The strong person is rarely rewarded early in a career. Like the rewards for many other positive qualities, the reward for going the extra mile may be delayed. Still, if you are really the person who goes the extra mile, your own self-knowledge will be reward enough. You will know that you can cope with whatever you need to do. Eventually, others will know that in a crisis, great or small, they can depend on you.

Learn on Your Own. You will be showing initiative by learning all you can about the business and your place in it. You also show initiative by finding additional tasks to do when your assigned work is finished, by taking courses to prepare yourself for promotion, and by going ahead with work that must be done even though it has not been definitely assigned to you. Learn how to think and act swiftly in emergencies, and do more than you are told to do. If new and unusual situations arise, aside from your regular routine, you should handle them.

You will show initiative if you are able to take another employee's place without detailed instruction. You should be able to apply what you learn in one situation to a similar situation. You will plan and carry out new duties with a minimum of help from others. You will attempt constructive, creative work.

Learn to handle all telephone calls adeptly and to arrange conferences to the satisfaction of both or all persons concerned. Experience will enable you to tell whether you should call your employer at home if an important customer appears unexpectedly.

If you are alert, original, and determined to see and use opportunities, you will learn to take advantage of situations by a display of initiative. The person who is enthusiastic about putting new ideas into effect does not say, "It can't be done." Nor does the person bother superior officers with trifling matters or wait to be told what to do. Nor will the person need to have work laid out or to be told repeatedly how to perform a task. Do not let new and unfamiliar situations upset you. Through the use of initiative, let them be stepping-stones to greater efficiency.

A beginner does have a lot to learn. People expect it. They do not expect the learning process to go on forever, though. The beginner who needs to be told something only once is considered unusually bright. The one who learns new routines and facts without being told is rare indeed. Everyone makes mistakes, but the beginner with a good work attitude seldom makes the same mistake twice.

Be Conscientious. Earlier it was pointed out that many personality traits are sometimes evaluated. However, different people evaluate traits differently. What is conscientious behavior to one employer may appear to be pure laziness to another. So remember to learn your employer's expectations, and be conscientious enough to build a good reputation.

In some work situations it seems that employees spend more energy and creativity figuring out ways to avoid work than they spend actually working. This seems to be a problem whenever several young people are working together without close supervision. It also occurs more often when people are involved in dull, routine work. But older workers and even executives can be found to play such games. Here are a few examples.

Waiting ten minutes for someone to help you proofread two pages of typed materials

Delivering a package that could be mailed instead

Going to someone's office for a conversation instead of using the telephone

Beginning coffee breaks and lunch periods early or finishing them late

Carrying on social conversations (on the phone or in person) during working hours

Doing your personal work (without anyone else knowing about it) during working hours

Working fast (and carelessly) so there will be time, after all the work is done, to read, sleep, play cards, etc.

Working slowly to make the work fill up the time available for it

Causing a situation that will bring the work to a halt (a broken machine, shortage of materials, etc.)

Daydreaming when you should be concentrating

Performing a task yourself when it could (and should) be done more efficiently by someone else

Wasting time preparing for or talking about doing a job instead of getting to work and doing it

Refusing to do something that you could do because "it is someone else's job"

Wasting a lot of time kidding around playing jokes or pranks on coworkers

Pretending not to notice customers waiting to be served

Some of these actions may, at times, be normal and acceptable. But any of them, when carried to the extreme, can cause your employer and coworkers to think of you as someone who wastes a lot of time. You probably have heard that time is money. Most employers see it that way and they appreciate the worker who refuses to waste it.

In addition to conserving and using time well, the conscientious worker is not content with doing a mediocre—or average—job. Doing a *good* job without wasting time—that's what most employers will expect.

QUESTIONS AND PROJECTS

1. What does it mean to be resourceful? Give examples.

2. What is the difference between "external" motivation and "internal" motivation? Give examples of each. Under which type of motivation is the most work likely to be accomplished? Explain your answer.

3. You ride the bus to work. The schedule allows you to arrive either 25 minutes early or three minutes late. What would you do?

4. List several ways you could improve your self-motivation. From the list, choose the ways in which you could start now.

5. Assume you have been promoted to supervisor. One of the people with whom you formerly worked is now working under you. Kay is habitually late for work; she is doing a good job otherwise. It is your duty to talk to Kay about her tardiness. What will you say to Kay? Write down your exact words.

CASE PROBLEMS

1. Job or Career?

Laura Montefiero is a salesperson in the clothing department of a department store. The sales staff in the store is paid a weekly salary. No commission is paid for the amount of goods sold.

Laura is very industrious and is usually the first to greet a customer. After serving her customers, Laura returns the clothing to the racks. She then keeps busy arranging merchandise or studying new items that have been recently put in stock. She is always pleasant and courteous.

Dale Salizar, who works with her, tells Laura she is foolish to work so hard when she receives no extra pay. Laura knows that Dale's attitude is characteristic of the feeling of many of the members of the sales force.

- a. Is it profitable for Laura to work as she does?
- b. Do you feel that Laura may be rewarded for her work attitudes?
- c. If Laura does not receive a promotion, can you think of any advantages her attitude would have?
- d. Why do you think the other clerks feel as they do about their work?
- e. If you were in charge of Laura's department, how would you handle this situation of indifference on the part of some of the sales personnel?

2. How Much Is Too Much?

Shirley supervises the shipping and receiving department of a university library. She has several part-time student helpers. Usually, they are able to keep up with the flow of incoming mail. However, after weekends or holidays the books and magazines pile up and it may take several days for Shirley and her crew to get caught up. Most Mondays and days after holidays Shirley works from one to three hours overtime to catch up.

- a. Since Shirley works on a salary, she gets no overtime pay. Should she continue working overtime? If not, how should she handle the situation?
- b. Shirley catches the flu and misses three days of work. When she returns she finds the backlog of undelivered mail so great that she has to work eleven hours per day for a week. Her supervisor does not seem to know about Shirley's overtime work. What should she do? At what point do you think Shirley should refuse to work overtime?

6

Developing Your Productivity: Work Habits

LEARNING OBJECTIVES:

1. Explain principles and techniques for organizing work.

2. Develop the ability to determine acceptable performance standards regarding amount and quality of work.

3. Learn to avoid losing excessive time on personal matters.

4. Learn to work under pressure.

5. Develop habits of neatness, thoroughness, and concern for accuracy.

Nadine met Gloria at the water fountain and they paused for a bit of conversation. "I can't imagine how Randy gets anything *done*," Gloria whispered, nodding in the direction of Randy's workspace. "He has stuff all over the place. And he seems to be in a dither half of the time, just keeping track of what he is doing." "I know," said Nadine. "And I overheard the supervisors talking about it, too. He seems *to get the job done*. But I don't know."

____ *Your* success in business will depend to a great extent upon your ability to develop good work habits. Inborn intelligence is highly overrated by many people as a factor in success. A brilliant mind helps, of course, but it will not ensure success. Interest in your work, enthusiasm, work habits, carefulness in checking details—all these play an important part.

You may have observed someone with great talent who was at the top of a profession. What you did not see was the long period of hard work that had gone into this person's career. The axiom that genius is 90 percent perspiration and 10 percent inspiration is true. Even gifted people must work hard if their talent and intelligence are to benefit themselves and others; work always requires self-control. In the long run, all of us want to work, but doing the job in front of us requires much personal discipline. If a supervisor oversees the work, this outside force helps you to settle down to work. If you have a job you must do without prodding from others, you must have the self-control to work efficiently.

ORGANIZE YOUR WORK

Another rung on the ladder in your climb to success is the ability to organize a task into manageable units. For example, if Job A and Job B are needed in order to do Job C, you should see that Jobs A and B are done first. Organizational ability becomes more important as you rise higher in your work level. When you take your first job, it will usually be a routine one. Someone else tells you what to do, checks your work, and suggests improvements. As your ability increases, however, you will find that you are trusted more and more to take care of the total job, to decide how you are going to attack the problem. Here is where you will need organizational ability.

Much of what has been discussed in the preceding chapters will help you become better organized: learning to make decisions quickly, seeing that your work output is high, developing accuracy in your work, and working within the acceptable standards of your job. Now, however, you must learn to do the hard job first. You must eliminate the common habit of putting off until tomorrow what should be done today. Secondly, you must see that all of the papers, drafts, tools, and so on, needed for a single job are kept in one place. This way, you will not be wasting time looking for the things you need when you start work on that job.

Organizing your work also means planning your work. You must make a plan before you start. If organizing is new to you, you should write your

ILLUSTRATION 6-1.
Organizational ability
becomes more impor-
tant as you rise higher
in your work level.

plan down. First comes the due date. Write down when the job must be completed. Next, divide your task into parts and set a date when each one is to be finished. Third, make sure all of the supplies, papers, answers to questions, and needed calculations are at hand. Then go to work. See that you work on the task the number of hours necessary each day in order to complete the job when it is due.

You may have heard of Parkinson's Law. It states that work expands so as to fill the time available for its completion. If you are invited to an exciting party and have just thirty minutes to finish up a task, you'll get it done in thirty minutes. If you have three hours in a lazy afternoon, somehow that same task will take three hours to finish. Knowing how to organize is the key to beating Parkinson's Law.

Step-by-Step

Here is a step-by-step procedure that may help you to organize your work:

Get a Clear Idea of the End Product. If you are following instructions from a supervisor, make sure you have understood all that you were told. If there is a written description of the job, study it carefully. It may help to write down a statement of the objectives or outcomes that you are to achieve.

Develop a Procedure.   The procedure consists of a step-by-step plan of action. It may be that your assigned task is not so complicated that you will need to consider several steps to accomplish it. However, if you think logically about it—considering what should be done first, what next, and so on—you will be able to visualize that start-to-finish procedure. Again, it may help to write down each step, along with key points to remember and be aware of as that step is accomplished.

Determine the Resources You Need to Accomplish the Task.   It may help to ask yourself, "What equipment, supplies, help from other workers, workspace, and the like, will be needed to get the job done?" A careful review of the procedure, asking this question at each step, will help you to develop a list of needed resources.

Obtain the Needed Resources and Take Care of Any Preliminaries. When you accomplish this, you will be ready to begin. You will have what you need available and you will have a plan of action to follow.

Follow the Procedure.   As you follow your plan of action you should be alert and aware of any important safety precautions, quality concerns, company rules and policies, and critical information about how to perform each step in your procedure effectively and efficiently.

Evaluate Your Work.   After you have completed the task, compare the product or results with your intended objectives or outcomes as specified in step one above. Did you get the job done well? Were the resources used as planned? What are the differences between what you *expected* and what actually occurred along the way? What are some ideas for improving your efficiency and effectiveness next time?

LEARN TO BE EFFICIENT

Haru Yamamoto and Kevin Melville were seatmates on an airplane trip to a travel agency managers' convention. Haru started the conversation. "How's business, Kevin?" "Best ever, Haru. But I'm a bit worried about how it's going to be after next week. My best agent has been hired away by Yamamoto World Travel!" Haru smiled. "I know. And I expect my business to improve. We're lucky to get Thelma. In your letter

> *of recommendation, you should not have been honest." "I wish we could have offered her a management position,"* Kevin responded. *"Thelma is the most* efficient *agent we have. Not the most intelligent. Not the best educated. Not the most experienced. But the most* efficient!*" What do you think are some of the specific skills that made Thelma so special?*

One of the most important work habits a worker can possess is efficiency. This means that, first of all, your workplace is arranged neatly. Study several examples of neat, efficient layouts. Notice how supplies should be arranged for quick and easy handling. A neatly arranged workstation will make *you* more *efficient.* You will be ready to plan and organize materials, supplies, and the work itself so that tasks can be completed as rapidly and as accurately as possible. Efficiency also involves discovering the work standards in your place of employment and working hard to meet them.

One difference between actual employment and school assignments will soon become apparent: Perfection is always desirable, but sometimes it must give way to practicality. For instance, if a letter is not centered, you might have to mail it anyway, because time and supplies might be more important than perfection. In other cases, such as machining a part to specific tolerances, you may have to throw away the spoiled part and start over. Being efficient involves judging the relative values of tasks when measured in terms of time, energy, and supplies. These judgments will vary, of course, according to the needs of your particular firm.

Step-by-Step

Following are some specific suggestions that may help you to be more efficient and effective in the performance of your job.

Keep Your Workplace in Order.   It may help to keep everything you work with in a certain place. If you find that you have supplies or equipment that you rarely or never use, find an out-of-the-way place for it, or get rid of it. Place those things that are most useful and often needed so that you can get at them easily.

Avoid Borrowing from Coworkers.   You will find that if there is something that you need and do not have, it is best to make an effort to obtain the item for your own use. The worker who constantly borrows tools or supplies from other workers will soon have trouble finding friends.

Strive for and Appreciate Accuracy. Accuracy and pride in your work go hand in hand. If you are accurate in your paperwork, you learn to check everything. You proofread carefully. If you are uncertain about a name or address, you look it up in the files or the telephone directory. If you deal with numbers, you check them carefully. Anyone can make an error; however, you are there to see that no error gets past you.

Be Thorough. If you are thorough, you finish what you start, you keep trying, and you follow through. When completing an assignment, and particularly at the close of a working day, you check to see that all details have been taken care of. If you do bookkeeping work, you see that each entry is carefully and correctly made. If you are involved in sales transactions, you make out all sales slips completely, accurately, and legibly. You see that all reports and correspondence are correct. If you have any doubts about the meaning or spelling of a word, look it up in the dictionary. Check the enclosures that accompany your correspondence. You make sure that every task entrusted to you is performed completely and accurately.

ILLUSTRATION 6-2.
Cultivate the habit of
being thorough.

Don't Put Off That Hard Job. You may think that today is too hectic to start a big, important job; you'll put it off until tomorrow when things will be better. But tomorrow will not be better. It might be worse. Say to yourself, "I'll just get started." Somehow, the momentum builds up from getting started, and you may get a big chunk of the job finished the first day.

Don't Be Distracted by Details. Don't be concerned about having everything just right before starting your work. You may be tempted to adjust the temperature or the lighting. You get a drink of water. You sharpen all your pencils. Don't allow yourself to waste time on such details. Get going and get the job done!

Don't Be Indecisive. You can waste time trying to get all the facts and deliberating endlessly over decisions that may not be all that important. There is a story of a farmhand, John, who was assigned to sort potatoes in

Florida Department of Commerce/Division of Tourism

ILLUSTRATION 6-3.
When you make time outside your work to do some of the things you enjoy, you are better able to work under pressure when the need arises.

the warehouse. After several hours of work only half a bushel had been sorted, and the farmer, Sally, confronted John, asking why he was taking so long. John's response was, "I don't mind the work, but it's the decisions that are killing me."

Don't Leave Your Workday to Chance. *Plan* each day the night before or before you begin your work in the morning. If you tend to be disorganized, you should write your plan. The mere act of writing something is a first step toward accomplishing it. Do not think only of the difficulties as you plan your day—how hard the job is, how tired you are, how little you are appreciated. This kind of thinking gets your unconscious mind working against you. Instead, visualize yourself accomplishing your work.

Suggest Improvements

Another habit that will contribute to your success is one that must wait until you have established yourself in your job. Even then, it is wise to make suggestions for improving work techniques tactfully. When you can make suggestions without offending other workers or your supervisor, you will have become a real asset to your company. New ideas are always welcome; the danger lies in suggesting your new ideas with a "know-it-all" attitude— and before you have really learned how to do your job efficiently. Remember, though, that business needs new ideas, new techniques, new ways to save time and money. Be willing to offer them without expecting anything in return.

Avoid Spending Time on Personal Matters

If you are interested in building a reputation for being efficient, you will take care of personal matters on your own time.

When you are at work, you will give your time and your attention to your job. One particular personal matter that should be considered is personal telephone calls. Your company may have strict rules regarding personal telephone calls during working hours. Even if it does not, you should refrain from talking to family and friends during your working day except in cases of emergency. If a friend calls you at work, tell the friend you will call back on your first break or during your lunch hour. If you are a working parent, you may find it necessary to take a personal call if it has to do with your child's welfare. When the need arises, however, try to keep the call short. Use a pay phone rather than tying up the business lines with personal matters.

Visiting with other workers should be discouraged, too. Of course, you will be friendly and pleasant. Greet other workers when you come to work in the morning and when you leave in the evening. But talking over last night's activities or your favorite sport should wait until lunch or break time.

Whatever the rule, do not spend too much time away from your work for any reason. You would not take money from the cash register; neither should you take time from your working day.

Keep Your Productivity Within Accepted Standards

Part of your job success is your ability to produce. Speed alone, though, is not the key to efficiency. The way to build up your work production has three parts: (1) an efficient workstation, with your tools within easy reach, (2) repeated practice on the parts of the task that slow you down, and (3) an objective that increases as you improve. For example, if you can lay only forty cement blocks in an hour, try to improve that rate by (1) having the blocks within easy reach and having enough mortar always on hand so that you don't run out. Then (2) repeat laying down just the right amount of mortar if leveling each block is a problem for you. Finally, (3) try to lay forty-five blocks per hour. Once you have succeeded, see if you can lay fifty blocks in an hour, and so on.

The same procedure can be used with any kind of work. Remember, though, that your objective must be to increase the amount of work while maintaining high quality of work.

Keep the Quality of Your Work Within Accepted Standards

Another test of efficiency is your willingness to keep at a difficult job until you get it right. Willingness to take pains with your work is not spread equally over all different kinds of tasks. For example, you may be happy to retype a page in order to make it neat and free from smudges and noticeable erasures. This same desire for perfection, however, may not work for you when you are asked to go through the files and discard papers that have outlived their usefulness. You may do a sloppy job if you are told to clean up the duplicating room.

Every job has some drudgery in it. You must be willing to take the drudgery with satisfaction. Be sure you have what it takes to become quality-conscious in your work. Pride in your work can be developed. However, it helps if you can find the kind of work in which you *want* to take pride—where quality is important to you.

Learn to Work Under Pressure

Finally, we call attention to one of the factors that contribute to your mental health—the ability to work under pressure or abnormal conditions. This means you are able to meet deadlines, keep three or four jobs going at once, and do extra work without panic. Of course, you will be better able to work under pressure if your physical health is good, but there is an added factor. Can you remain calm in a crisis? One way to build this added factor is to learn to control your emotions. Sometimes when pressure mounts, it helps to stop for a moment (especially when you feel your muscles tightening up) and take a few deep breaths. Other times you may find it helpful to do a relaxing exercise: swing your hands at your side and drop your head forward. Relaxation is the key, and many of us must train ourselves in relaxation. If you can find time outside your work to do some of the things you enjoy, you will be better able to work under pressure when the need arises.

Productive work habits are nothing more than ordinary habits applied to work. Once you learn how to make your habits work for you, you will become more productive in your job and more valuable to your employer. Chances are you will even feel better about yourself as well as your work.

QUESTIONS AND PROJECTS

1. The text mentions the fact that young people, especially when not closely supervised, are likely to waste time. What are some possible reasons for this? As a supervisor, what might you do to overcome this problem?

2. Imagine that you are working in a situation where just as you are assigned to do three different jobs—all to be done right away—a critical piece of equipment breaks down. How would you handle such a crisis?

3. You work in a situation where coworkers are expected to fill in for each other when someone is absent from work. In what ways might you prepare for the time when you will be assigned to fill in for someone else?

4. You are assigned to a new job in the accounting department. You are told that the chief accountant, your supervisor, is a perfectionist. What implications does this information have for you? How might you go about learning what standards of performance are expected of you?

CASE PROBLEMS

1. Take Up the Slack.

Martin Brady and Marion Stuart are employed as billing clerks by a merchandising firm. When Martin is asked for certain invoices, he has to rummage through his files before he can find them. He does, however, make out all invoices neatly and accurately. Marion, who occupies the next desk and does the same kind of work, uses a system. He makes notations about invoices that cannot be completed at once and is constantly trying to find shortcuts and timesaving devices.

Martin is always joking with Marion about the latter's "efficiency." Martin tells Marion that he really does not produce more work than he does. However, Marion is promoted to the bookkeeping department to a position that has more responsibility. Martin believes that favoritism is being shown.

    a.   What businesslike attitudes does Marion show that he possesses?

    b.   In what ways does Martin show he is not businesslike?

2. Room at the Top?

Tad has obtained a subordinate position in an advertising firm. In high school Tad capably handled all the advertising copy for the various school publications. He feels, therefore, that his experience fits him for doing creative work, and he is not interested in the tasks assigned to him. He considers them to be dull, routine duties. The manager knows that because Tad cannot do the type of work he wants to do, he often neglects to do well the work he has to do. Tad's negligence also causes more work for others in the office. They, in turn, complain to the manager. When Tad is called to the manager for questioning, he explains that he does not like his present tasks and tells of his ambition. She does not seem to be impressed with his reasoning.

    a.   What is your opinion of Tad's attitude toward his work?

    b.   If you were the manager, what would you say to Tad?

    c.   Why did Tad's ambition fail to impress the manager?

    d.   Have you observed this attitude toward starting at the bottom in other lines of work? Explain.

    e.   Why was Tad's attitude not fair to the other employees?

3. Future Dividends.

Ted Tyler was employed as one of two bookkeepers in a small manufacturing concern. Midge Christopher was the manager of the accounting department. Ted found that he could work much faster and more accurately than his fellow employee. He thus had time to spend in doing extra work or in helping the other bookkeeper. Things seemed to go just as well, however, if he took more time with his own tasks. He worked more slowly, therefore, so he would not have to do anything extra.

At the end of the year some special reports and records had to be prepared. Henry Mack was employed as an extra bookkeeper for one month. Although his work was temporary, Henry was interested in the job and worked as hard as he could, doing exceptionally well. At the end of the month, when Henry was scheduled to leave, Midge became ill and had to resign. Midge recommended that Henry be given her vacated post as department manager. This was done.

    a.   Do you feel Midge was justified in overlooking Ted's seniority in the firm?

    b.   Do you think Ted had any claim on the position as department manager?

    c.   In working slowly, what impression did Ted give Midge as to his ability?

    d.   If Ted had worked more efficiently and then spent the extra time in helping the other bookkeeper, would this have gone unnoticed?

4. Who Is Responsible?

Claire Baker usually proofreads all letters after she transcribes them. Her employer dictated several letters at 4:15 p.m., and because Claire was in a hurry to leave, she mailed these letters without proofreading them. In one letter that asked for the payment of a past-due account of $50, she typed the amount $40 in full payment of the account. Claire's employer insisted that she make good the difference. Claire agreed, but she thought the demand was very unfair.

    a.   Who is responsible for errors of this type, the business or the employees who make them?

    b.   What is the rule when cashiers make mistakes in giving change?

    c.   Why does business insist on accurate records where money is involved?

    d.   What opinion might the customer who paid $40 have of the firm?

5. Cluttered Desk.

Jasper Matsura has a basket on his desk marked for incoming work. He has asked his supervisor several times to place any work for his attention in this basket, since his desk tends to get cluttered because of the many interruptions through the day. Nevertheless, his supervisor repeatedly comes in asking for work that Jasper has never seen. When he looks through the accumulated piles of paper on his desk, Jasper finds the requested items.

    a. Do you think Jasper has handled the problem correctly? Why or why not?

    b. Can you think of another way of handling the problem?

6. Quotas at Work.

Some companies set work production quotas for their employees to meet. At times, these quotas may be met by working less time than the normal working day. Or it may be possible to meet the quotas by working extra hard for a few hours only.

    a. If you could meet your quota in just six hours (of an eight-hour day), should you just waste time the other two hours?

    b. Do you think production quotas are fair:
       1. To employers?
       2. To employees?

    c. Should you improve your job performance if you are already meeting your quota? Why or why not?

7. Use of Initiative.

Frank Zwiefel has just completed a report that must be sent out in the afternoon mail. His supervisor, Jill Green, intends to send a letter with the report, but she is called out of the office just before closing time and without having been able to dictate the letter. Jill says nothing to Frank before leaving. Frank knows, however, that the letter will be similar to the one sent the previous month. He decides to type the letter and sign it with Jill Green's name and his own initials.

    a. What would you have done in Frank's position?

    b. Which would be more serious, sending the letter without being told or sending the report without a covering letter?

    c. If you were Frank's employer, how would you react to having an employee act in this way without instructions?

7

Working with Coworkers

LEARNING OBJECTIVES:

1. Describe the personality traits conducive to working with others.

2. Emphasize the importance of being a team player.

3. Point out the "don'ts" of being a team player.

4. Explain the principles of group behavior.

Edith had been employed as a dispatcher for a trucking company for several years. She did her job efficiently. She was considered a conscientious and hardworking employee. Her coworkers, however, felt that she was a loner. She didn't seem to be able to fit in. Edith was passed over for a promotion she thought she had earned. She decided to ask her most trusted coworker, Miguel, to help her understand why she was not selected. Miguel attempted to explain to her in a tactful way that she was not perceived as a cooperative member of the working team. If you were in Miguel's position, what suggestions would you give to Edith? Why didn't Miguel offer these suggestions to Edith before she was passed over for promotion?

___$Many$ studies show that your ability to succeed in the workplace depends upon how well you get along with your coworkers. On the job, getting the work done is a team effort. Therefore, the reasons why it is important to get along with your coworkers are obvious. You will enjoy your work more if you have a good relationship with your fellow employees and the productivity of the working team will be improved. The supervisor, of course, is also an important member of this working team. The importance of establishing an appropriate relationship with the supervisor is discussed in Chapter 8.

KEYS TO GETTING ALONG WITH OTHERS

Employees are hired because they have specific skills and knowledge to get a job done. They are not hired because they have like interests, personalities, backgrounds, etc. Therefore, establishing a good working team is not always an easy task. No two people are alike. Those you work with may perceive things very differently than you do. They may have values, habits, traits, and personalities that are different or in conflict with yours. It is hard to develop a team spirit in a group of people who may be very different but who are assigned the same tasks.

There are some personality traits or characteristics that will help you get along well with your coworkers. These key traits will help you become a member of a working team. Your efforts to become a member of the team may be rewarded in several ways—you will be working in a pleasant environment, your productivity level will be improved, and your chances for a pay raise are more likely.

Cooperation

The first key to working with others is to be cooperative. **Cooperation** is the ability to work smoothly with others. It is going out of your way to be helpful to others. Cooperation is like a bank account. It may not pay immediate dividends. Yet, if deposits are made, the dividends will eventually become both frequent and of a high rate. Like a bank account, too, cooperation may demand that you give up short-term conveniences for the sake of future rewards.

You must earn the reputation for cooperation. You will earn it by thinking not of your immediate comfort, but of the ultimate welfare of your organization and your customers. Cooperation is actually an expression of self-interest and unselfishness. It demands that you adjust your immediate pleasure to the best interests of others. Yet the reward for immediate sacrifices is a reputation for cooperation, which will contribute to your success.

Cooperation may be a simple act of sharing your materials or equipment with a coworker. It may mean helping to cover the territory of another salesperson who is unable to do it alone. It may mean willingness to go out of your way to help a customer or coworker. It may mean holding back when you want to disagree, being a good sport when you have lost a sale, or showing tolerance in listening to the ideas of others when your own ideas seem superior.

In almost any career, you will be expected to cooperate many times and in many ways. You will need to keep your workplace and belongings neat and tidy, assume additional duties and assignments without complaint, work overtime when there is a need, and offer your services even when you are not obligated to do so. You should surrender your own ideas if they do not fit in with the policy of the organization. Tell others of devices that may help them and show unselfishness whenever you can. You should pass on your ideas and the results of your own experiences to others. Listen when others try to help you with their ideas and the results of their experiences. Work harmoniously with others to advance the interests of the organization.

Politeness

Little words like "please," "thank you," and "good morning" are very powerful in the work environment. These comments of politeness let others know that you care about them and appreciate them. Laurie has had a particularly difficult day. Her alarm didn't go off. The dress she had planned to wear had a spot on it. She missed her bus. As she walked in the door, she was greeted with a smile and a cheerful "good morning" from her coworker, Alex. This greeting may turn around the unpleasant events of the morning for Laurie. Alex's politeness contributes to a cooperative working atmosphere.

Patience

It is important for you to remember that not everyone will catch on to routines at the same rate. Remain calm as you help a coworker with a new process. Be patient when coworkers ask questions in a staff meeting that you think are unnecessary. A less than patient attitude may quickly lead to conflict and a negative work environment. Sam was explaining to a new employee, Tom, the procedures for ordering supplies for the office. The procedures were somewhat complex and required a knowledge of which

ILLUSTRATION 7–1.   Not everyone catches on to routines at the same rate.
Remain calm as you help a coworker with a new process.

wholesalers and retailers carry which products. As Tom was new to the business, he was not familiar with the vendors in the area. After Sam had completed his explanation, he asked Tom if he had any questions. Tom had several. Sam answered the first few questions with a degree of patience. After that his body language and tone of voice let Tom know that Sam was irritated. Finally Tom said, "If you didn't want to answer my questions, why did you ask?" Sam followed up with, "You don't seem to know anything about this business. Why do you want to work here?"

An explosion like this one is very damaging to a good work environment. Sam and Tom lost their patience. Much repair work will need to be done before Sam and Tom will be able to get along as coworkers. The other workers in the area will need to work together to get Sam and Tom to remain members of a good working team.

Enthusiasm

Enthusiasm is a very contagious feeling. If you are enthusiastic, it seems to spread to others. There is an old saying, "If you think enthusiastic, you will be enthusiastic, go-o-o-o enthusiasm." This is certainly a positive and true thought. People who are enthusiastic have an inspiration for their work. They show positive and true enjoyment for what they are doing. If you are inspired and eager about your work, this will often cause everyone to get work done more quickly and easily. Tricia said, "I don't know how I'll ever get this report out. It is dull work and will take hours." Jerry was always full of enthusiasm and eager to get work completed. Jerry replied, "I think if we work together, we can polish off that report in no time. Let's get to it and get it completed and move on to more pleasant tasks." Jerry's enthusiasm and spirit of cooperativeness will, we hope, spread to Tricia, and the report will be produced.

If you do not look forward to going to your workplace and cannot express genuine enthusiasm about your job, look for other employment. You will be doing yourself and others a great favor.

Dependability

Teamwork is based on the ability of one worker to depend upon another. Think of mountain climbing teams. The life of one climber may depend upon the actions of another. Their work together as a team is built upon dependability. The same is true in the workplace. Another key to getting along with coworkers is your ability to be dependable. Can your coworkers count on you to be punctual? Do you have a good attendance record? Do you complete tasks on time? Do you follow through on requests? Can coworkers depend upon you to assist them if they get overloaded with work? These questions point out just a few of the qualities required of a dependable coworker.

Loyalty

Connie continually made negative remarks about her coworker, Frank Rutcosky. She said that Frank flirted with customers, wasted office time, and was inaccurate in his work. Frank overheard some of Connie's remarks about him in the canteen during a break. He confronted Connie with her comments and a conflict began.

It is important to be loyal to the people with whom you work. Loyalty to the business and your supervisor is also important. If you possess business information that should be kept confidential, keep it to yourself. Loyalty and faithfulness to your workplace is key. If you are not proud to introduce your coworkers to others and promote the place where you work, you may be in the wrong job.

An effort to be cooperative, polite, patient, enthusiastic, dependable, and loyal will go a long way as you work to get along with coworkers. As you develop these characteristics, you will set an example for others. Remember, it is not fair to expect others to demonstrate the key traits unless you are willing to exhibit them also.

YOUR POSITION ON THE TEAM

Teamwork is based on the key traits of getting along with others just described. Think of yourself as playing a certain position in your organization's team.

You may be keeping records. If you are, make sure that these records are accurate and thoroughly checked. If you are a shipping clerk, see that your position is filled perfectly; see that there is no slipup in your part of the team play. If you write the first draft of a report, check the information that goes into the report. Do your very best to see that the report is written as well as you can do it. Remember that, like the player in a football game who throws a forward pass, you pass your part of the report to the person who will write or dictate the final draft. That person will make the touchdown. You will be the team member who makes it possible for someone else to catch the ball and carry it over the line. You can see why, as a worker, you *must* understand why people behave as they do. Machines may supply facts and figures, but people still make the business enterprise go—or break down. One person can create enough friction to make it break down. You must make sure that *you* are not a behavior problem, but you must also learn to understand others when they are.

Don'ts of Being a Team Player

As you think of yourself as a team player, keep in mind that there are some "don'ts." There are some pitfalls which you should carefully avoid.

Don't Take Advantage of Coworkers. It will be necessary at times to ask a coworker to assist you in some way or take care of some of your assigned responsibilities. However, you should never take advantage of another or shirk your own work. Mary Beth was a new checkout clerk at a large discount store. After several days on the job, she was feeling very comfortable with her work and her coworkers. Frank was especially helpful to her during those first rough days. During Mary Beth's second week, Frank explained to her that he needed to make a very important phone call. He asked Mary

Beth to cover his checkout station during her break. Mary Beth was happy to help out. Mary Beth was somewhat concerned, however, that whenever she had an opportunity for a break, Frank needed help at his station or completely left Mary Beth with his responsibilities. It is obvious that Frank was taking advantage of a new employee. This type of arrangement is not conducive to teamwork. When someone does assist you with your work, be sure to thank them and return the favor whenever possible. It is not necessary, however, to allow someone to take advantage of you.

Don't Speak Before You Think. You should feel comfortable about expressing your ideas when you think they are appropriate suggestions. It is important to use good judgment in deciding when you should speak up and when it is better to keep silent. There may be some situations which you should protest, but you should also listen to the ideas of your coworkers, supervisors, or perhaps even customers. Many times they will see a perspective which you may have overlooked. If a decision is made and your ideas are overruled or rejected, you must abide by the decision in a cheerful manner.

So much depends on speaking—when to speak, when not to speak, what to say, and what not to say—when working for advancement. It is true that sometimes silence is golden. A beginning worker, for example, should be slow to suggest changes in working procedures. Before you make such suggestions, you should study the reasons for the present processes. You might learn from such study why your changes would not be practical at the moment. Suggesting changes just to prove you are alert and up to date is a practice that can only be detrimental to you.

When you do decide that speaking up is important, come directly to the point. If explanations are essential, organize them in a logical form. State your case and answer the questions which result from your comments. It may be that your employers will welcome your suggestions. If, however, you find that your supervisors have different ideas on the subject, you should respect and abide by their decision. It will not be in your best interest to argue or refuse to cooperate. The main thing to keep in mind is that you *think* before you speak.

Don't Let Your Emotions Get Ahead of You. The word *think* is important not only when you are preparing to speak. Thinking is also important to keep your feelings and emotions intact. Even the best of us cannot hope to be 100 percent objective—even part of the time. There is a good possibility that we do things, and say things, for unconscious reasons. We must be on guard for this possibility. If we are promoted to a new and difficult job, for example, we may find ourselves in a state of panic. If you should find yourself in this position, don't expect to find sensible reasons for your fears. They may be caused by an excessive desire to be perfect. In other words, you may be afraid of failure and not afraid of the job. You may be able to cure your panic by telling yourself that mistakes will almost surely occur at first. The expected, you see, is not so frightening as the unexpected, and you may find your fears disappearing.

Don't Make Hasty Judgments About Others. Understanding the possible reasons for others' behavior will keep you from making unfair hasty judgments about coworkers. If Craig's desk is next to yours and he challenges everything you say, it may be tempting to stop speaking to him altogether. You may find yourself avoiding conversation with him, but this will not solve your problem. It will not help build teamwork. It would be a good idea for you to attempt to figure out why Craig feels the need to contradict and challenge your comments and decisions. In Craig's case, he may feel inferior to you. He may feel extremely insecure in his position. Craig may have no idea how to seek help for real or imagined inadequacies. You can help by providing reassurance now and then. Your help may stop the challenges he has been tossing at you.

Don't make hasty decisions about the actions of others. They are struggling along in life just as you are. Sometimes unattractive personality traits cover up a tendency that is their exact opposite. The clown may be unhappy; the braggart may be insecure; the person who laughs too much may be

ILLUSTRATION 7–2.
It benefits you and your firm when you take the initiative in the friendly greeting, the approving word.

shy; the excessively sweet person may be covering up a true dislike of people. Give others a chance before passing judgment.

Everyone has these same needs. Your employer, who may seem to be the ultimate in success to you, may feel completely unappreciated. In fact, the higher you climb on the ladder of success, the more lonely you may become. It will help you and your firm if you take the initiative in the friendly greeting, the approving word. No one gets too much appreciation. If you are able to show your appreciation of others, you can make a good start in building a better psychological climate around you.

If you are committed to a greater understanding of others, the next step is to keep from being a behavior problem yourself. It is better to be positive, to be cheerful. Now, let's talk about how you can understand, get along with, and even help others to fit in as members of a working team.

UNDERSTAND AND USE GROUP PSYCHOLOGY

In almost every workplace there are at least two people, and two people make a group. If you work now, or if you plan to work someday, you must learn as much as you can about the psychology of groups. What makes *groups* tick? How does our group behavior differ from our individual behavior? Why is it so important?

Group behavior is important because whatever you do affects the way someone else in your group feels. When your actions make others feel positively toward you and toward the group, you help others do a more effective job. When your actions cause friction and bad feelings in the group members, you will hold them back from doing their best work. Thus, your actions will diminish the effectiveness of your group. The problem, then, is to work on yourself, to be the kind of person who brings out the best in people in the group, not one who contributes to the problem that so often exists when people work closely together.

Help the Problem Coworker

Even if you personally do not create problems in your group, do you do anything to *help* those who do? Many groups have members who drive everyone else up the wall with personal insecurities, negativism, or closed minds. There are two things you can do to help the problem person in your group. First, you can tell about some problem you had when you first joined the group. (Most of us go through an adjustment period when first joining any kind of work or social group.) You can go to the difficult group member and tell what a hard time you had in adjusting to so many different personalities. You can tell the person how inferior you felt when everyone else seemed to be so much more competent than you. This is one sure way to help the difficult group member open up to you. When the person tells you some of the troubles experienced with the group, the troubles become less troublesome. The second thing you can do is comment favorably on something that made the work go more smoothly, that helped get things done. If you do this, you will be working to make the group a real one, because real groups are made up of real people. By showing another person the real you, you help that person become more real, too.

The theory behind changing a group so that it works better is called *shaping*. If you can get some of your friends to help you shape the difficult group member, you can accomplish some remarkable results. Shaping means that you pay no attention to the irritating things the group member does, but you give reward or praise for the things said and done that are helpful. Most of the difficulties people have when they become a part of a group are caused by lack of confidence. Praise is a good confidence builder.

The first step, though, is to be a real person yourself. You must be willing to feel and express real feelings. If someone says something to you that makes you feel happy, say so. Say, "That makes me feel wonderful!" If someone says something to you that hurts you, you will be a real person if you can say, "I wish you wouldn't tease me about that. It's something I'm kind of sensitive about." If you say something like this in a straightforward manner, without whining or accusing, you will show the other person a part of the real you. You will remove part of your mask. In most cases, the other person will respond in the same way. Of course, such statements are hard to make. It is much easier to sulk, to go away, or to refuse to talk to the other person. But these actions do nothing but make matters worse between you and the other person. Every bad relationship in a group hurts the group as a whole and makes it less effective in getting things done.

When you want to help make a change in your coworkers, you must proceed indirectly. You cannot call all of your fellow workers together and say, "Look, let's all be real. Let's all try to accept one another." When you do something like this, the rest of the group will wonder what you are after. People do not like to be forced to do things—even if they are for their own good. Shaping works best when the technique begins with you. When you are more real in dealing with your coworkers, that realness becomes contagious. Some of your fellow workers will catch realness from you. Someone else will catch realness from your fellow workers. In an organization where everyone is real, no one needs to wear a mask to cover one's real self. Work no longer seems like work in such an organization. It becomes a very pleasant activity.

How to Talk with Complainers

Every group has one or more complainers. You may find yourself in the listener role for the complainer. If you wish, you may take this role as a compliment. The complainer can be a very dangerous member of the working team. The complainer is more damaging than the other characters in the work group because complaining can be highly contagious. It is important to feed the complainer with very positive and cheerful statements whenever possible. Whatever you do, don't let the complainer influence your thinking so that you become a complainer, too.

When others come to you with their complaints and troubles, you may often attempt to minimize the other person's troubles. Some of the standard lines are, "Now is your problem really that serious?" or "Don't take everything so hard." This technique does not often work because the complainer may feel that you have a heartless attitude and are not willing to listen.

ILLUSTRATION 7–3.
Complaining can be contagious. It is important to feed the complainer with positive and cheerful statements whenever possible.

Another technique to consider is simply to repeat what was said, but in different words. Suppose the complaining coworker says to you, "I am sick and tired of being treated like dirt by Abernathy. I have had enough of him pushing around his authority." You need to come up with a comment which will help to calm the complainer down. "I can tell Mr. Abernathy has made you angry." This technique is an attempt to put the person's feelings into words. By doing this, you let the complainer know that you understand the *feelings* behind the complaints. You are not saying that you agree with the feelings or that you condone the outburst, but that you do understand.

Counseling psychologists use this technique of reflecting back on what the person has said. It is commonly called a **nondirective approach.** The approach is often effective in dealing with complainers, as it eliminates our tendency to give advice, to preach, to take sides, or to defend the complainer. The nondirective method also has positive benefits for the complainer. It draws out negative feelings and provides an opportunity for the complainer to pause, take stock of the situation, and think it through.

The same technique is especially effective when the angry person is aiming that anger at you. The same kind of response is the best one. When a coworker yells at you, "How can you be so clumsy!" you answer calmly, "I don't know. I just seem to be a bit careless at times. I'm sorry." Admitting your own faults to the accuser is almost guaranteed to eliminate the anger in the accuser. The only problem is that you must keep all traces of sarcasm from your voice as you give your calm reply. Bad feelings and conflict between people don't just happen; they are caused. Without knowing it, you may be part of the cause. If you can take the giant step of admitting your part of the cause of the trouble, you will help the other person take the equally hard step of admitting to a share of the blame.

Every working group has its stock characters. These may be recognizable at once, or they may be hiding behind a false front. This is one reason why you should take your time in joining one of the many groups you will encounter. The secret of a successful entrance into a new employment situation is to be pleasant with everyone. Say "Good morning" to the janitor, the president, and everyone else.

Other Characters in the Work Group

Along with the problem coworker and the complainer, you will encounter other characters in a work group. The following paragraphs describe these characters and give suggestions on how you may interact with them.

The grouch.   Every group has a grouch. The grouch may upset the beginning worker. Remember, though, that the grouch is not mad at you. In fact, the grouch may have a lot of respect for coworkers and supervisors. The causes of the grouch's behavior are generally unrelated to work. Problems at home, physical problems, or financial troubles may cause the behavior. Also, some people get into a grouchy mood for little or no reason and seem never to have an interest in changing their behavior. If you are pleasant and caring, and refuse to take the grouch's complaining personally, you may make such a person become less of a grouch.

The tattletale.   Another dangerous character is the tattletale. You can recognize a tattletale by the stories told you about other employees. Do not tell your own stories about other employees, no matter what the provocation— even if you hear what one of the employees said about you. A tattletale will go back to this person and repeat what you have said. Gossip is unwise at any time, but gossip with a tattletale is positively dangerous. When such a person starts telling you some tale about another person, be polite but firm. Suddenly remember a pressing engagement. There are plenty of your coworkers who will listen, unfortunately. The tattletale will leave you alone if you refuse to listen.

The bossy "non-boss."   What about a bossy "non-boss"? There is usually one around. This person criticizes everything you do (and everything others do, too). Remember that bossy people are mainly dissatisfied with themselves. Calling attention to the faults of others is just a way of trying to feel satisfied with themselves. Pay no attention to the bossy person who is your coworker. If such a person *is* your boss, however, you will help by paying careful attention to detail and by following directions as accurately as you can.

Don't Become a Character Yourself

There are two other characters in the work group, and you should avoid assuming the role of either.

The favorite.   You may want to become the favorite employee. No. Try to avoid this title if you can. If the supervisor seems to favor you, you will have to work extra hard to stay on good terms with your coworkers. It is important not to capitalize on such favoritism. Continue to treat your supervisor with respect and a formality that indicates respect.

The arguer.   Another character you must not assume is that of the arguer. It is possible to avoid unnecessary arguments. It takes only two ingredients, relaxation and patience. If someone makes a controversial statement, relax. Feel your muscles go limp. Then wait and listen until you have heard the whole story. Many arguments are merely the result of not letting the other person finish. Decide to say nothing until your "opponent" has talked for at least three minutes. By that time, particularly if you are relaxed, you will find yourself much less likely to say something rash, something that might hurt the other person's feelings.

SPIRIT OF SERVICE

Everything that is done in one department is usually of service to some other department. Records are kept, papers are filed, plans are made, and products are produced, all to serve the company as a whole. Any worker, then, must be service-conscious. You must be willing to do all in your power to make the company run smoothly. To fit, you must be willing to serve. The typical workplace is no place for the temperamental person.

To recognize the importance of a service attitude, imagine that you are a member of a bucket brigade engaged in putting out a fire. A long line of people pass the buckets of water along the line from the stream at one end to the fire at the other. Suppose you drop the bucket when it gets to you? What will happen to the group effort? This is how important each member of the working group can be.

QUESTIONS AND PROJECTS

1. Use the nondirective approach with someone you know when they complain to you. Write up the situation. Record the situation, your non-direct comment, and the reaction of the complainer.

2. List the five characteristics you would most like the person working most closely to you to have. Compare your list with others. Rate yourself on each characteristic on a scale of one to ten. List the qualities that you have which would make you a good coworker.

3. Find or develop cartoons which depict the "grouch," the "complainer," and the "bossy non-boss."

4. This chapter emphasized that making incorrect assumptions about people can be dangerous and lead to conflict. What assumptions have you made about others which turned out not to be true? Did your assump-

tions lead to conflict? How did you discover that your assumptions were not accurate?

5. John works in a fast-food restaurant. He is so enthusiastic about his responsibilities that he steps all over his coworkers in an attempt to get to the customers first. He doesn't notice the negative reactions of his coworkers. If you are one of John's coworkers, how would you handle this problem?

6. The way to avoid argument is to relax and wait for the whole story. The next time you are tempted to argue with someone, say nothing. Just be patient and listen. Write down the results of your experience. Did you accomplish anything? Do you feel this is a helpful solution for you?

7. What action would you (as a coworker concerned about getting along) take? Harriet has worked at the Harvard Shoe Company for the past week. On Friday some of the women go out for lunch. They don't ask Harriet to join them. Harriet should:

_____ Run after the group and ask to be included.

_____ Send them a memo and ask why she wasn't included.

_____ Be patient and give people a chance to get to know her better before taking any action.

8. A birthday party for the supervisor is being planned. A sheet with all the employees' names on it is being passed around. People mark whether or not they plan to attend. Donovan is a new employee. The sheet is passed to him but his name isn't on it. Donovan should:

_____ Tell the person who made up the sheet that his name was forgotten.

_____ Add his name to the list and mark whether or not he plans to attend.

_____ Assume that he is not wanted at the birthday celebration.

9. Few of us could live happily without friends. Try the following steps in winning new friends:

a. All day Monday smile at those you meet at school or at work. Praise at least one person you greet.

b. On Tuesday relay a kind or encouraging word to every close associate you talk to during the day.

c. On Wednesday seek out someone in need of a friend and invite that person to do something with you.

d. On Thursday choose a stranger to talk with, discussing only that person's affairs—not yours.

e.   On Friday write a friendly letter to someone.

Evaluate the experience of the week. Do you feel more friendly with someone? Has anyone made friendly overtures to you?

CASE PROBLEMS

1. To Cover or Not to Cover.

Les Burton, one of your coworkers, has been asking you to "cover" for him while he takes extended lunch breaks. In addition, he leaves his desk for 30 to 45 minutes during peak telephone hours. You make every attempt to answer his calls, but sometimes it is difficult. Today, he called in before the office opened. He asked to speak to you. Les said that his car broke down and he will be late for work. He asks you to "punch in" for him so that he will not lose any pay.

   a.   Will you punch in for Les? Why or why not?
   b.   Is Les violating any of the basic rules of working with others? If so, what are they?
   c.   Should you discuss this situation with Les? With your supervisor? If so, what would you say to Les? What would you say to your supervisor?

2. Making Change Easy.

You have just become employed by the Brunimaker Company as an assistant to the purchasing agent. You will be spending most of your time in the stockroom area with your coworker, Clyde Brown. Clyde has been with the company for 25 years. He established the system of records in the company. This system is outdated, clumsy, and difficult to use. You recognize that the old system needs to be updated. Your major concern is how to get Mr. Brown's cooperation in making the change to a more efficient system.

   a.   How will you win the confidence of Mr. Brown?
   b.   Write down the opening statement you will make when you bring up the matter of installing a new record system for the first time.
   c.   Assume that you win Mr. Brown's cooperation. What will you say when he makes a suggestion that you feel is not a good one? Give the conversation in detail.

3. Work Team Importance.

Rosita is a part-time employee in a savings and loan company. She hopes to have the opportunity to move into full-time employment very soon. She has been fairly successful in her part-time job. She is accurate, reliable, and conscientious. She spends very little time communicating with coworkers and avoids the attempts of others to include her in activities taking place outside office hours. When she is asked a question, she gives quick answers and drops the conversation. A full-time position opens up in the company. Rosita's supervisor is asked if she thinks Rosita should be considered for the position. Her response is, ''She is a good producer, but not a team player.'' The position is offered to someone else. Rosita is very upset.

   a.   Should Rosita make an attempt to find out why she was passed over for the position? Who should she talk to?
   b.   If you were her coworker and found her in the hallway in tears following the decision, what would you do? Say?
   c.   Does Rosita's supervisor have a responsibility to her to point out why perhaps she was not considered for the position?
   d.   Why do you suspect that Rosita does not make the effort to become a member of the work team?

4.   New Employee—New Idea.

Ted is a new salesperson at the Aldrich Department Store. He is working in the men's clothing department with five other employees. Ted was informed that all price tags were to be saved and then sorted at the end of the workday. It took approximately twenty minutes to sort the tags. Ted felt this was a stupid process. He developed a box with punched holes in it that made it easy to sort the tags after each sale. He presented the process to the other employees and said that they should begin using it immediately. The other employees did not accept the idea since they liked getting in the extra time after work. They also felt that it slowed down the selling process and took time from the customers. Ted and his ideas were ignored. Ted didn't like this type of treatment and quit.

   a.   Did Ted (who needed a job) do the right thing?
   b.   Was the new method of sorting a good idea? Why or why not?
   c.   How could Ted have gained acceptance of the new idea?
   d.   What steps could Ted have taken to be accepted again as a part of the sales team?

8

Getting Along with Your Supervisor

LEARNING OBJECTIVES:

1. Explain the basic management styles.
2. Understand the importance of relating to your supervisor.
3. Develop an ability to take a problem to your supervisor.
4. Realize the expectations of your supervisor.
5. Explain the importance of seeking, accepting, and handling deserved and undeserved criticism.

> Jan and Carol work for an independent insurance agent, Ms. Campbell. Ms. Campbell is very busy and out of the office most of the time. She relies on Jan and Carol to take the phone calls, process and file claims, answer correspondence, and handle all the typical office operation details. Ms. Campbell gives general directions when she has a few minutes to spend in the office. Jan enjoys her work very much; she likes the freedom to make decisions and do things "her way." Carol is very unhappy working for Ms. Campbell; she resents having to make decisions which she feels should be made by her supervisor. She frequently comments, "I don't get paid enough to assume the responsibilities forced on me in the absence of my

> boss." She is never sure just exactly what is expected of her.
> What recommendations would you have for Carol? How can
> one person be so happy in an agency while another doing simi-
> lar tasks in the same setting is so unhappy?

_No matter how good you are at what you do, your chances for job success and promotion are reduced if you cannot establish a solid working relationship with your supervisor. Your future in the work world may hinge on your ability to get along with the person who makes the decisions of hiring, retaining, and terminating personnel.

Getting along with your supervisor doesn't mean apple-polishing, conniving, or manipulating to assure that you are in good standing with her or him. It means making a conscious effort to manage your relationship so that it achieves the best possible results for you, your supervisor, and the organization that pays both your salaries.

KNOW YOUR SUPERVISOR

A supervisor, for discussion purposes in this chapter, is defined as a person who is in charge of a group of workers. Supervisors are unique individuals. They have feelings and needs similar to your own. It is important to realize this as you begin to establish a relationship with your supervisor. Your supervisor may be a football fan, a cook, an avid reader, a distance runner, a tennis player, or a songwriter. Like all of us, supervisors have strengths and weaknesses, good days and bad days, hopes and fears, and special personality quirks. They are skilled at some things and not as good at others. It is important for you to learn to understand and respond to your supervisor as a real person. He or she is someone who likes some things, doesn't like other things, and doesn't much care about still other things. You will get along better if you make a positive effort to accept and respect your supervisor as a unique human being.

Management Styles

Each supervisor has a basic way of managing people which he or she uses to accomplish the goals and objectives of the organization. The different ways of getting the work done are called management styles. It is im-

ILLUSTRATION 8–1.
You get along better
when you make a posi-
tive effort to accept and
respect your supervisor
as a unique human being.

portant to become acquainted with the various styles of management and recognize the one selected by your supervisor. Once you understand your supervisor's management style you will have taken an important first step toward developing a good working relationship.

The three basic management styles are: (1) autocratic, (2) democratic, and (3) *laissez faire* (a French word meaning to let alone). Each style has its own set of characteristics.

The Autocratic Supervisor.

The **autocratic supervisor** dictates procedure, policy, and tasks to employees. This style of management clearly identifies the supervisor as a leader and the employees as followers. The autocratic manager tells employees what work needs to be done, how it will be done, and when it will be done. The employee is usually not consulted or asked for ideas. A person who uses this style may not be comfortable in delegating authority. To delegate authority means to entrust an activity, decision, or responsibility to an employee.

If you are the type of individual who feels comfortable in taking direction and is eager to be given a specific job assignment, you may enjoy working for a supervisor who uses the autocratic style of leadership. The following story may help you better understand the autocratic leader.

Ms. Stine is the supervisor of twelve men and women employed in the word processing center of a large insurance company. She is very proud of the work of the center. She refers to the employees as "her" operators and the center as "her" department. She gives specific instructions about the number of lines to be processed per day, the precise number of break minutes allowed, the lunch schedule, the style of production that is acceptable, and the dress code. She does not ask for employee suggestions when changes are made in the organization. Each worker in the center is informed in detail about his or her responsibilities and duties. Ms. Stine is an autocratic supervisor with a reputation for getting the written communication of the organization out in short turnaround time.

To perform successfully under the supervision of an autocrat, you will need to remember that you are in the role of a follower. You will need to be patient, cooperative, accepting, and reliable to function under the autocrat. It is also very important that you carefully follow directions and adhere strictly to the rules, regulations, and policies of the organization.

Autocratic supervisors are not comfortable with the employees who exhibit traits like initiative, creativity, and assertiveness. These traits are threatening to some supervisors using this style of management and should be avoided.

The Democratic Supervisor. The **democratic supervisor** uses a very different approach. He or she may suggest what to do and how it should be done, but the employees are encouraged to participate in the management process. Democratic supervisors like to exercise only a moderate degree of control over the employees. They have confidence in their employees and seek input from them. They encourage employees to participate in the decision-making process, explain reasons for policies, procedures, and changes, and enjoy talking over work-related activities and problems with workers. This style of leadership is often referred to as participatory management.

If you are working in this type of setting, your ideas will be sought and you will be encouraged to see yourself as a part of a working team. Meetings will be held so that your thoughts and ideas can be heard. Committees may be established to develop employee suggestions.

Here is an example of what might happen under the democratic management style of Diane Olson. Diane has established a specialty chocolate shop and employs ten people. She is a very proud entrepreneur and is eager for the shop to be a profitable venture. Diane holds employee meetings on a regular schedule to get ideas and opinions from the staff on pricing, advertising, and providing for the wants and needs of the customers. She recognizes the value of her employees' suggestions, as they hear the customer's comments on a daily basis. The employees determine their own break and lunch schedules based on customer traffic. They helped Diane establish a fair sick leave policy, an adequate employee insurance program, and a profit-sharing program.

If you feel your thoughts are worthy of consideration and you like the idea of contributing to the success of an organization, you will enjoy working for a democratic supervisor. In this setting you will be expected to contribute ideas, help solve problems, and be an important part of the team. Workers in a democratic leadership environment are expected to be creative, enthusiastic, cooperative, and empathic, and to show initiative.

If you feel your only commitment to the work environment is to do your specific job, and you prefer to leave the decisions (for which you are not paid) to the supervisor, this is not the managerial style you will enjoy.

The Laissez Faire Supervisor. The **laissez faire** style of management sets a policy of "hands off" in dealing with employees. Supervisors who use this style exercise little or no control over the employees. While this style might bring chaos in some work settings, it is excellent for others—especially those businesses requiring maximum creativity from employees. The *laissez faire* manager avoids giving specific detailed directions, permits employees to work independently, encourages initiative and creativity, and provides only general guidance.

This style works well for the employee who enjoys freedom and likes working in a creative environment. The worker is given a free rein to get his or her work accomplished and receives little direction from the supervisor.

ILLUSTRATION 8–2. The laissez faire style of management is excellent for those businesses requiring maximum creativity from employees.

Employees working in this environment get the work completed as best they can using their creative talents and relying on their past experiences.

Susan and Marc Owen use the *laissez faire* style in operating their small advertising enterprise. They employ two technical writers, several artists and graphics personnel, and a marketing specialist. Susan and Marc explain the needs and wants of their clients to the staff and charge them with the task of developing a campaign to fulfill the requests of clients. The artistic staff provides the graphics for the advertising campaign, the writers provide the copy, and the marketing person determines the media to be used in the campaign. The staff members work out their own schedule of communication and product development.

If you have creativity, initiative, self-confidence, assertiveness, self-discipline, and the ability to set your own goals, you will do well under this type of leadership. You will be successful in the *laissez faire* approach if you act independently, devise your own solutions, and make your own plans and decisions. You will want to check in with your supervisor periodically to make sure that you are moving in the right direction.

Each management style has its advantages and disadvantages. You should recognize that a supervisor may at times use a mixture of styles in order to accomplish a goal of the organization; however, there will continue to be an underlying style. When you become angry or unhappy with your supervisor, ask yourself the question "Is it the supervisor who angers me, or is it the management style?" Chances are it will be the style—being angry with the style saves you from being unhappy with the supervisor. If you find there is one management style under which you work best, work towards getting yourself in a setting where the supervisory style suits your skills, needs, and work habits. Remember, the supervisor's style will probably not change. It is your job as an employee to adapt to the style of your supervisor.

In addition to being aware of your supervisor's management style, you also need to study your supervisor's world. Take the time to sit down with your superior and get an idea of what his or her objectives and responsibilities are. You need this information to do your job efficiently and effectively. You do not want to be pulling in the wrong direction. This will also give you the opportunity to let your supervisor in on your personal and professional goals.

KNOW YOURSELF

As you concentrate on knowing your supervisor, you are reminded to review the chapter on knowing your inner self. Have you ever received a gift that you didn't like very much and had to force yourself to react appropriately to the giver, but eventually grew to really enjoy, use, and appreciate the gift? The friend who gave it to you may have perceived something about you that you did not know about yourself.

If you learn about your strengths, weaknesses, and general work style from some of the people with whom you work closely, you may find that they perceive things about you that you would never quite notice about yourself. All of us have blind spots, areas of our personality which we do not see clearly. Find out what your blind spots are by questioning your supervisor. This will strengthen your relationship with her or him and it can help you to strengthen your character.

Know what you are doing. Take your position seriously. Educate yourself about the "state of the art" in your area. Keep track of what's going on outside your own department, division, or branch as well as what's going on within it. By cross-training yourself, you can become more knowledgeable about your own area and more aware of how it fits into the scheme of things. What does this have to do with getting along with your supervisor? Well, the more you know, the more useful you can be. When your superiors recognize that you are working at developing personal and professional competence, you are more likely to receive opportunities to grow and be promoted.

In an effort to become better acquainted with yourself, check to see if you have the characteristics most desired by supervisors. Are you a **diligent** worker? A diligent worker is one who does what is expected and more. Supervisors notice those who are willing to do extra or unpleasant tasks. Diligence is a trait which pays off when the supervisor has an opportunity to give pay raises and promotions.

Do you show an **allegiance** to the organization for which you work? Workers who show allegiance to the organization by telling outsiders about the products or services of the company, keeping quiet about problems of the organization, and supporting the goals and objectives of the organization. Avoid the temptation to denounce, betray, or bad-mouth your supervisor or company. If you cannot be proud of your workplace, it would be best to seek other employment.

Are you **honest** in your dealings with the supervisor? Honesty has many sides—it means not stealing goods from your employer, putting in an honest day's work, giving 100 percent effort, and telling the truth whenever questioned. Many employees have been fired for taking company tools, materials, or property. Using company stamps or the postage meter for a few personal letters may cost you your position or eliminate your chances for advancement.

Are you **enthusiastic** about your work? Many supervisors feel that the best employees are those who like their work and show enthusism for it. When you enjoy your work, life itself will be more interesting and you will be a happier person. All jobs have some unpleasant tasks. Don't dwell on the tasks you dislike. Focus your thoughts on the positive parts of the job which you enjoy. When someone asks you about your position, tell them about the good things. By focusing on and sharing the positive parts of your job you will be a more productive and successful employee. The reason supervisors feel enthusiasm is so important is because enthusiasm is contagious.

Keep in mind that when you are hired it is expected that you will contribute to the growth and success of the organization. Your relationship with the supervisor will blossom if you work to develop the above listed characteristics and in doing so contribute to the growth and success of the organization.

RELATING TO YOUR SUPERVISOR

In an attempt to establish a solid working relationship with the supervisor, you must have an open line of two-way communication. Two-way communication offers an opportunity for you to respond to an employer directive and vice versa. The following tips will help you to establish a good rapport with your supervisor.

Allow no surprises. Any time there is a crisis, a problem, a potential problem, or a new development in your area of responsibility, make sure that your supervisor hears about it from you first. Having your superior hear about a catastrophe in your area from someone else can be very detrimental to your relationship with the supervisor and could be terminal. Keep your supervisor apprised of what is happening. Your supervisor cannot be in all places at all times; therefore, communication from you is essential.

Know your supervisor's preferred communication style. Some people prefer information in writing backed with facts, statistical data, and other supporting documents. If your supervisor prefers this style of communication, use it. Write a memo, letter, or report. If your supervisor is a listener and likes to hear reports and react immediately, then make it a practice to pass along information verbally.

Be a good listener. To understand what your supervisor wants from you, you must be a sharp listener. When you are discussing a topic, listen carefully, not just for what the supervisor is saying, but for what she or he means, and for what implications it might have. If you are not getting the supervisor's "drift," restate what has been said. After the discussion, summarize what you have learned in a few sentences to make sure you understand each other.

Take problems to your supervisor. It is important that you be able to take problems to your supervisor. This process requires thought and preparation on your part. Before you consider taking a problem to the supervisor, be sure that the problem is worthy of the supervisor's time and attention. After this determination has been made, you are ready to begin the appropriate steps of presenting the problem. These steps follow:

1. *Establish a suitable setting.* You are sharing a problem with your superior not the entire work force. Step into a private office, a canteen area, or a quiet hallway. This will help insure that you have the ear and attention of the supervisor.

2. *Explain the problem in your own words.* Use terms that accurately describe your concerns and feelings.

3. *Present facts that support the problem.* These facts should be carefully gathered prior to your problem presentation. Do your homework! Your facts should be specific, documented, and accurate. You will lose credibility by stating half truths, generalizations, and innuendos. Avoid using phrases like "I hear that . . . ," "I assume . . . ," and "Rumor has it . . . "

4. *Ask for understanding.* Pause . . . and ask your superior if he or she understands the problem. (Notice that you have been assuming a leadership role in this process.) This pause will also allow your supervisor to ask questions or clarify points that you have made.

5. *Present several alternative solutions.* This indicates to your supervisor that you have given thought to the solutions. Again, do your homework prior to your presentation.

6. *Identify your recommended solution.* Indicate the solution which you think is the best solution; however, by no means suggest that your recommendation is the only alternative.

7. *Thank your supervisor.* Thank the supervisor for the time and attention. Suggest that you would like to follow up.

After you have completed this seven-step process, return to your workplace and resist the temptation to share with coworkers your conversation with the supervisor. The employee who is skillful in communicating with a supervisor has an edge over coworkers who do not realize the importance of this skill. You will increase your communication skills by studying Chapters 12 and 13.

WHAT DO YOU HAVE THE RIGHT TO EXPECT?

Research and observation indicate that the relationship between the supervisor and employee is improved when there is a good reward exchange between them. If you provide productive service and allegiance to your employer, you have a right to expect freedom to work with a minimum of supervision, job security, a safe working environment, and personal recognition. As an employee, you have a right to expect certain things, as does your supervisor.

After studying parts of this chapter which discuss the expectations which the supervisor has of you, you may be getting the feeling that you are expected to give a lot and not get much in return. This is not so. You do have a right to expect certain things from your supervisor. The list would include, of course, wages, safe working conditions, and training. In addition, you should also expect explanations for decisions, clarifications of policies, fair evaluations of your work, honesty, and suggestions. If your expectations are reasonable but you are seldom on the receiving end of the reward exchange, you may want to follow the steps of taking a problem to your supervisor and bring your thoughts and needs to the attention of your employer.

Your Right to Criticism

The right to receive criticism from your employer is a fair expectation. You may respond to that statement, "What do you mean, why should I want to seek out criticism?" The reality is that we all need criticism. Criticism should not be thought of as negative. Criticism is a form of **self-improvement** and should be regarded as such. Without criticism and suggestions from your supervisor you will be unaware of how to improve. No matter how skilled you become on the job, improvement is always possible. Improved skills lead to additional self-confidence, promotions, and income.

Many employers will avoid the task of providing you with adequate criticism during performance evaluations and other appropriate opportunities. When constructive criticism is not given, your employer is doing you a disservice. Why is it that employers withhold criticism? Employers find the task of giving criticism to be very difficult and unpleasant. Think of yourself as a future employer—it is doubtful that administering criticism will be one of your favorite duties. Other more specific reasons for bypassing criticism responsibilities are:

1. Many employers feel that if you work at a job long enough you will figure out what is being done wrong and correct the problem. The

employers' attitude is let them alone and they will work things out for themselves.

2. Employers prefer not to raise the ire of the employee. If things are going well, they take the attitude "why bother to upset anybody?"

3. Employers may fear an emotional reaction on the part of the employee. Some people do not take criticism well and respond in an emotional way. Reactions may be pouting, crying or even a loud emotional outburst.

Therefore, unfortunately, supervisors may not choose to risk the consequences of giving criticism. You are the loser when this decision is made. You will not be given the benefit of information which will help you become a more productive worker.

It is important for you to let your employer know that you appreciate and can accept criticism. This can be done by asking your supervisor questions about your job performance. Speak up during performance evaluations and ask for suggestions on how to improve. Whenever comments are shared about your work, accept the comments in a positive manner and thank the supervisor for the interest in your success.

Reactions to Criticism.   Avoid the negative ways in which people often react to criticism. Some employees become defensive and offer excuses. This is a natural tendency and we all do it. If a friend says, "You are a grouch today," a typical human response might be, "Well you would be a grouch, too, if you had the problems I have." In the workplace excuses continue. "There are errors in the report because my work area is so noisy." Responses such as this are certainly not ways to indicate to your superiors that you can handle criticism. A better response about errors in a report would be, "Thanks for pointing those out, I'll correct them right away."

The attack is another negative response to criticism. Attackers focus the spotlight away from themselves and put the blame on someone else. "I did a lousy job on that job because Clara didn't give me specific directions about how you wanted it done." The attacker does not handle criticism well and may be creating unnecessary conflict with a fellow worker. A better response in this situation may have been, "I didn't understand the directions about how this was to be done. Please review them with me and I'll try it again."

Others react by withdrawing, feeling guilty and inadequate. Those who react in this manner ask no questions about how to improve, but rather give up and take the "what's the use" attitude. This type of behavior is obvious to your supervisor. Again, you will be the loser, as the supervisor may not want to deal with this attitude in the future.

ILLUSTRATION 8-3. Criticism and suggestions from your supervisor can help you be aware of how to improve.

If you usually react to criticism by defending yourself, by attacking others, or withdrawing, you are experiencing a lot of emotional pain without much healing. When you fail to use criticism to your advantage, you may suffer the loss of self-esteem and work improvement.

Handling Criticism. The positive method for handling criticism is first to evaluate it. Is it deserved or undeserved criticism? Handling deserved criticism is of course much easier. Try the following steps with *deserved* criticism:

1. Listen very carefully to the suggestions being made.
2. Ask questions if necessary to clarify the error which you made or the suggestion being offered.
3. Offer to correct the error if possible. Pledge an effort to try suggestions.
4. Thank the person giving the criticism.

You then leave the situation with your self-esteem in place and get back to your work. Your supervisor will recognize that you can accept criticism and be willing to communicate recommendations to you in the future.

Coping with *undeserved* criticism requires more courage and control. At some point in your career you will be unfairly criticized; it happens to everyone. A series of steps should be followed carefully to deal with this unfortunate situation:

1. Listen carefully to your accuser. Do not interrupt. Do not try to deny. Don't say "but," "wait a minute," or "no." Just keep quiet.
2. After the criticism has been expressed, ask polite, reasonable, and responsible questions about the situation. It is not necessary to be rude or raise your voice. Keep calm.
3. Lead your accuser through your questions to the fact that you are being unfairly criticized.
4. Accept the apology of the accuser, if one is offered. Keep in mind that apologies for some people are very difficult and none may be forthcoming.
5. Say "thank you for your time," if you can possibly squeeze out the phrase.
6. Return to your workplace and keep your mouth shut about the incident.

Above all don't keep a chip on your shoulder and don't take on the attitude, "Well I guess I got that straightened out."

Let's review a scenario of how not to deal with undeserved criticism. Ann has worked part-time for Dr. Georgi for several months. The job is very important to her and she enjoys the work. Dr. Georgi is the Foreign Language Department Chairman at the University. Ann seldom sees him as she gets her work assignments from his secretary, Wanda Comstock. Dr. Georgi calls Ann into his office. He says, "Young woman, sit down!" He directs her very sternly to a chair. Shaking his finger at her he says, "You just cost the University $2,000." He tosses a letter at her. It misses her lap and she leans over to pick it up. By this time, she has a large lump in her throat and tears are streaming down her face. She tries to blurt out, "I don't understand. What's the problem?" Her words are garbled because of her emotional state. He says to her, "This letter offers an assistantship to a graduate student; you typed in the figure $6,000 rather than $4,000. This guy is a smart cooky and he has sent us a telegram stating that he will accept the offer of $6,000 as stated in our letter." Ann is now recovering somewhat and she looks at the letter. She realizes while scanning the letter that she did not work on the day the letter was typed, she doesn't recognize the name of the recipient, and, most importantly, the reference initials at the bottom of the page (WC) are not hers. She sobs, "I didn't type the letter." Dr. Georgi replies, "Well, how do you know that?" She tells him. His retort is, "Oh, I see. Well, I'd better talk to Wanda about this." Ann is upset for the remainder of the day and is concerned about the wrath that is about to come down on Wanda Comstock.

Unfortunately, Ann was unaware of the prescribed steps for handling undeserved criticism. She should have:

1. Listened carefully and calmly to Dr. Georgi's accusations. Remained emotionally in control. Picked up the letter and scanned it.
2. Asked him, "On what date was the letter typed?" "Whose reference initials are on the letter?"
3. Let Dr. Georgi know that she is not guilty.
4. No apology was offered so she can skip this step.
5. Say, "Thank you for your time. I hope this situation has been straightened out."
6. Returned to her desk with dignity intact.

Handling undeserved criticism is tough and takes practice. The rewards however are great. It is important to your relationship with a supervisor that you be able to demonstrate an ability to accept criticism.

(By the way, Ann asked Wanda later in the day what happened. Wanda said, "After listening to him, I just said 'Who signed the letter?'")

Criticism can help you take off the blindfold blocking out your weaknesses. If you approach criticism positively, you will find that criticism can be as valuable as praise. You are probably aware of your strong points. It is important to allow others to bring out your shortcomings.

QUESTIONS AND PROJECTS

1. What questions would you ask a supervisor in an effort to get to know him/her as a person?

2. Arrange to interview a person who works in a supervisory capacity. Use the questions you prepared for number one.

3. Write a memorandum to a supervisor who prefers written communication. Tell the supervisor about a coworker who has an idea on how to improve the packaging of the cookies your company manufactures. The coworker doesn't think her idea is worth much, but you are convinced it will save the company dollars. Your job is not to describe or sell the coworker's idea, but to encourage the supervisor to quiz your coworker about her idea.

4. Under what management style would you prefer to work? Why?

5. The following phrases describe characteristics of autocratic, democratic, or *laissez faire* management style. Identify the style which is being described. Be prepared to defend your answer.

    _____ Encourages original work.

    _____ Calls frequent employee meetings.

    _____ Seeks advice of all employees.

    _____ Does most of the decision-making based on his or her thoughts and research.

    _____ Wants to hear about all problems.

    _____ Provides little direction for the work unit.

    _____ Likes to have decisions made by the staff.

6. What do you anticipate will be your style of management? What do you perceive to be the strengths and weaknesses of that style? Why do you think this style will be yours?

7. List five businesses or industries in which you think the *laissez faire* management style would work to the advantage of the organization.

8. Employees working for a supervisor using the democratic style are highly motivated. Write a paragraph indicating whether you agree or disagree with this statement.

9. Step number three in explaining a problem to your supervisor is to present facts that support the problem. Choose the statements from those following which would be appropriate in communicating to your supervisor the fact that you are having a difficult time in getting to work on time because of the schedule of your family. You want permission to begin working at 8:15 a.m. rather than 8:00 a.m. You are willing to reduce your lunch break by fifteen minutes for this consideration.

YES	NO	
_____	_____	I hear that Theresa in the accounting department begins her workday at 8:15 a.m.
_____	_____	I was late three to five minutes every day last week.
_____	_____	My youngest daughter begins her classes at 7:45 a.m.
_____	_____	Our neighborhood does not yet have school bus service.

_____ _____ My spouse's hours may be changing in
                       another month or two.
_____ _____ Rumor has it that we may go on flex-time in
                       the near future.
_____ _____ I think the phones should be covered at least
                       during part of the usual lunch hour.

10. Why is it important for you *not* to make a point of discussing with coworkers conversations you have had with supervisors?

11. The chapter points out five characteristics to strive for in getting along with supervisors (allegiance, diligence, honesty, enthusiasm, and a willingness to learn). What other characteristics do you feel would strengthen your relationship with supervisory personnel?

12. Have you ever received undeserved criticism? What were your feelings? How did you handle the situation? Write out the situation and what should have been said using the steps of handling undeserved criticism found in the chapter.

CASE PROBLEMS

1. No Promotion.

Alice is the administrative assistant to the personnel manager, Miss Bergman. She has good skills, a positive attitude, and a pleasant personality. Alice enjoys having lunch with friends and frequently forgets the time and arrives back in the office a few minutes late from lunch. She often socializes with people from other departments and takes a few extra minutes at break time. However, her work is always completed accurately and in a timely fashion.

Miss Bergman is aware that Alice takes time which belongs to the company. Alice's performance evaluations are positive but when a supervisory opening for which Alice is qualified becomes available she is not considered.

a. What suggestions would you have for Alice's work habits?
b. Do you think Alice should have been considered for the supervisory position based on her job performance?
c. How can Alice put herself in a position to be considered for advancement the next time an opening is available?

2. Questions of Allegiance.

Frank is a bank teller in a small community. He is an accurate, steady, and dependable employee of the bank. Competition is keen among the three small banks in this rural setting. Frank stops for coffee each morning on his way to work and visits with friends and neighbors. Frank frequently mentions errors which are made in the bank where he works. He talks about the bank president's "shady" deals and speculates that some of the loans being made are a bit "shaky." Frank has a tendency to get carried away with his comments and now and then stretches the truth to gain a little extra attention.

    a.   What do you think about Frank's comments?

    b.   What characteristic of a good employee is Frank missing?

    c.   What may result if Frank's supervisor overhears the comments from the coffee shop?

    d.   What impression is Frank leaving with his friends and neighbors about his place of employment?

3. Change of Supervisor.

Sara is a good food service employee in a restaurant known for fine food and excellent service. Sara's job is to prepare spectacular desserts for banquets and parties at the restaurant. She has quite a flair for decorating cakes and enjoys using her creative talents to make each dessert extra special. Sara has worked under the supervision of Pierre L'Enfant for several years. Pierre has not supervised her work closely but frequently pays her compliments based upon comments from guests. Pierre retires and is replaced by Jack McCue. Jack closely supervises Sara's work; he is very concerned about the amount of time Sara devotes to each creation. He has set maximum amounts of time to be spent on the preparation of desserts, and each dessert requires his approval before being served. Sara is frustrated with Jack and is thinking about finding employment elsewhere.

    a.   What is the main source of Sara's frustration?

    b.   Would you encourage Sara to find employment elsewhere?

    c.   What will the impact be on the restaurant if Sara leaves?

4. Constructive Criticism.

Dan O'Casey has the habit of saying "you know" in every conversation. In fact, he sometimes repeats this meaningless phrase twice in one sentence. Peter Nabor, who works at the desk next to Dan in the credit department of a large insurance company, has noticed how Dan's repetition of the phrase annoys their supervisor. Peter decides to mention the matter to Dan. He tells Dan, however, that the mannerism annoys him— rather than mentioning the supervisor. Dan is hurt by the criticism and shouts loudly, "I do my job around here. My speech patterns are none of your concern."

    a.   Did Peter do the right thing in mentioning the mannerism to Dan?

b. Should Peter have told Dan that the mannerism was annoying to the supervisor?

c. What do you think about Dan's reaction?

d. What would have been a more appropriate reaction? Assume that the criticism was deserved.

e. Role-play with someone this situation. The actor playing Dan should follow the recommended steps for handling deserved criticism.

9

Coping with Conflict

LEARNING OBJECTIVES:

1. Explain the reason for conflict.
2. Explain the different types of conflict.
3. Identify the stages of conflict.
4. Identify the positive and negative ways of dealing with conflict.
5. Explain the attitude and steps necessary to solve conflicts.

> Mr. Hiedtbrink, your boss, is a very busy man. He is one of those people who always seems to be in high gear. Often, when you have a chance to communicate with him about a problem or situation, he gives you the impression that he wishes you would hurry. He indicates that he is listening, but you're not sure that you ever have his full attention. On Monday you stop by his office and indicate that two of your coworkers (Marcia and Ted) are involved in a conflict over job responsibilities. Your coworkers are valued, highly skilled, and well-trained employees of the company.
> On Tuesday, Marcia walks off the job and leaves a letter of resignation after a verbal conflict with Ted. Mr. Hiedtbrink is

furious that such a valuable employee has quit. He calls you in and criticizes you for not keeping him informed of problems and conflicts in your area.

What would you say to Mr. Hiedtbrink? How many conflicts are tucked into this case problem?

___*If* you were to see the single word **conflict** on a huge billboard along a highway, you might wonder for many miles what that word meant. Why was it there? What message was it suppose to convey to you? How were you suppose to feel? Whose message was placed before you?

CONFLICT: A WAY OF LIFE?

Usually when you see or hear the word "conflict," your thoughts turn to experiences you have had which you consider conflicts. Perhaps your thoughts turn to a fight you had as a child, an argument you have recently experienced with a coworker or friend, a court battle which you have read about in the paper, a war between countries, or a labor dispute in the community. Unfortunately, the word "conflict" usually brings to mind unpleasant situations or memories.

Why does the word "conflict" bring a negative message to mind? It negative thoughts because conflict generally occurs when a person's behavior interferes with or threatens another. Behavior that is different than yours may clutter up or cause confusion in your life. This will, of course, happen often. We all have our own likes and dislikes, habits, and personalities. There will be no end to conflict in your life, but the good news is that there are many ways to cope with conflict and actually change situations for the better.

Perhaps the word "conflict" was placed on the highway billboard in an effort to have you think about the importance of learning to cope with conflict.

CAUSES OF CONFLICT

As conflict is the clash of opposing attitudes, behaviors, ideas, goals or needs, it is a rare person who can get through a single day without experien-

PERSONALITY DEVELOPMENT FOR WORK

ILLUSTRATION 9–1.   When you find yourself in a conflict over a fact, try to solve it immediately by checking a source.

cing conflict. The first step to living with the realities of conflict is to recognize its basic causes.

Simple Conflict

Simple facts can sometimes cause a conflict. You and a friend may come into conflict over whether Dustin Hoffman has won two or three Oscars for his performances in motion pictures. A conflict over facts can be easily solved by looking up the fact. If you find yourself in a battle over a fact, try to solve it immediately by checking a source. Don't let a simple piece of information hurt a friendship.

Ego conflict

Your **ego** is your feeling of self-worth. If you consider yourself somewhat of a football expert, you may perceive conflict over a statement you made about football as an attack on your self-concept. Once the ego becomes involved in the conflict, the conflict will become more intense. Ego conflicts can be damaging to personal and employment relationships. These conflicts are damaging because the people involved may view winning or losing the conflict as a measure of personal worth.

False Conflict

Conflict which truly does not exist can appear to be very real. This type of conflict is called false conflict. Suppose you and a coworker agree to finish a report before leaving the office. Yet before the report is finished, your coworker begins to straighten up her desk and walks out of the room. You may feel betrayed, angry, or confused by her actions, and the feelings of conflict begin. You do not feel that the report can be finished if your coworker leaves the room.

False conflict exists when you believe that two goals cannot be achieved at the same time. When your coworker returns to her desk after a stretch break down the hall and resumes working, the conflict disappears. The first thing to do when you feel a conflict coming into place is to determine whether that conflict is real.

Value Conflict

Each of us has our own set of personal values. You have determined what is important to you. The values you have placed on certain aspects of life may not be the same as those of others. When the differences are brought into focus over a particular issue, conflict can occur. For example, you may feel that welfare is necessary to take care of certain members of our society. A friend may be very opposed to any type of program which involves the giving of government money to an individual. If you and your friend are to get along, you should probably seek areas of discussion which do not include the topic of welfare or agree to debate the topic for good verbal fun. In order not to risk further conflict, you should each recognize that you are not likely to change the other person's values.

THE STAGES OF CONFLICT

All of the above types of conflict may occur on the job. Conflicts among workers are very destructive in the workplace because they can destroy the morale of the people involved, divert energy from the important tasks which need to be performed, increase stress, and reduce the cooperative team spirit. Therefore, it is appropriate to examine the cycle of a conflict further. Regardless of cause or kind, conflicts typically go through a series of stages. It is important for you to be aware of these stages. As you think through the stages of conflict, you begin to realize how truly damaging and time-consuming a conflict can be in the work environment.

When a conflict in the workplace involves two individuals, it doesn't take long for others to learn about the situation. As a tense situation between individuals develops, the first stage of conflict unfolds—**taking sides**. The tendency is for everyone in the workplace to take the side of one or the other persons involved in the conflict. This can often split the workplace right down the middle and lead to little or no productive work.

The second stage of conflict is **keeping score**. The teams which have now developed often keep track of what the other team "does to them." During this phase each side tries to prove the other is unreasonable. They may even begin "keeping score" on behavior that is not related at all to the original conflict.

This leads to the third and potentially damaging phase—**the showdown**. Eventually, the people involved in the original conflict or the teams that have developed since will decide that they "have had it" or they "just can't take it any more" and decide to confront the other person or team. This can be done in a destructive manner by threatening each other physically or verbally or using some other negative technique of handling conflict. Or they can confront each other by some constructive activity involving talking the situation over and coming to an agreement or compromise.

The last phase of handling conflict is **adjustment.** After the showdown, one or both sides may decide to make some changes in their behavior. The adjustments that people make determine how well the conflict is settled. For example, if only one side makes the adjustments, the conflict may start all over again.

It should be noted that in some cases conflict can be constructive. This happens when conflict opens up issues that are important. Opening up issues can lead to clarification. Another positive result from a conflict can be that it helps build a spirit of teamwork among people as they share the conflict, celebrate its settlement, and learn more about each other in the process.

HANDLING CONFLICT

You now have an understanding of the types and stages of conflict. Now you need to become more aware of some of the ways adjustments in conflict are typically handled in our society. There are several negative ways of dealing with conflict, and they are often used. These negative techniques will be explored first.

Negative Techniques

A very common negative way of handling conflict is to avoid or withdraw from it. This means that you remove yourself physically or psychologically from the situation. This is typically done by staying away from a person, changing the subject, refusing to think about a conflict, or maybe even something as drastic as quitting a job. This can be very frustrating and difficult because your focus is on avoiding a conflict rather than on solving it or learning to live with it. Arturo told Yvette that the letter style she used for formatting Mr. Brown's letters was very dated. Yvette was hurt by the remark. She now avoids Arturo. She walks to a different bus corner to avoid seeing him. She changed her break time in an effort not to see him. If Arturo is mentioned in a conversation with coworkers, Yvette walks away from the group. She has rearranged her life over a conflict which could easily have been resolved. Avoidance or withdrawal is a negative and self-damaging way of handling conflict.

Another way you can deal with conflict is to delay the conflict. You may settle a small part of the conflict but not handle the very important issue. The excuse you use is that you are cooling off the situation temporarily. This method is not entirely negative. Sometimes postponing a discussion over a conflict gives it a new perspective and allows the people involved to calm down. However, this method of handling conflict may be negative if the delay is so long that the problem begins to increase.

Bill and Jose work closely in the shipping department of a local lumber yard. Bill and Jose work long hours to see that customers' orders are filled accurately and on time. One Friday evening Jose is anxious to get home to celebrate his son's birthday. A large order comes in for roofing supplies at 4:00 p.m., and Bill and Jose recognize that it will take them at least three hours to assemble and ship the order. Jose says, "I have worked sixty hours already this week. I am tired of all this overtime, and I'm going home at 5 p.m." Bill replies, "I cannot get this order out alone." Some unkind remarks fly back and forth between Bill and Jose. Mr. Rudolph steps in and offers to help Bill get the order out, and Jose goes home. The conflict then was temporarily settled. A small part of the conflict was handled. However, the real issues need to be handled in the near future.

The most negative way of handling conflict is by aggression. Through aggression you attempt to force another to accept your ideas. Aggression may be physical or verbal. Aggression is an emotional reaction to conflict.

ILLUSTRATION 9-2.
The most negative way
of handling conflict is
by aggression—physical
or verbal.

Lloyd and Fred are coworkers in a grocery store. Fred tends to spend too much time visiting with his friends who stop by the store. On one particularly busy Saturday, Lloyd says to Fred, "Come on. Let's get these shelves stocked." Fred replies, "Can't you see I'm talking to Sylvia?" Lloyd then takes Fred by the arm and pulls him toward the stocking area. Fred takes a swing at Lloyd and a fight follows. This form of aggression is obviously not going to get the shelves stocked, and both parties may have placed their jobs in jeopardy.

Verbal aggression can often be just as damaging as physical aggression. Kim says, "I don't know if I feel up to tackling this report today." Her supervisor replies, "This report must go out today. If you don't feel up to it perhaps I can find someone who does." Kim is very threatened by this response—as well she should be.

With both the physical and verbal aggression, the response is neither resolved nor discussed.

A Basic Problem Solving Method

None of the techniques discussed in the preceding paragraphs are positive ways of solving or resolving conflict. The negative methods were reviewed because they are often the techniques used to attempt to solve conflict. Now it is appropriate to turn our thoughts to some positive ideas about dealing with conflict.

Conflict surely keys an emotional response by all of those involved. This emotional energy needs to be channeled toward a constructive solution to the conflict. There are a few key attitudes that must be taken by the participants in a conflict if it is to be resolved positively.

If you are involved in a conflict and wish to resolve it, you must:

1. Choose to cooperate.
2. Believe that the problem has a solution and think about the positive results for that solution.
3. Recognize that a difference of opinion is beneficial. A difference of opinion is not an attack on an idea or person.
4. Respect the opinion of all involved regardless of their position in the workplace, personality, or level of experience.
5. Make an effort to be patient.

Once these attitudes are in place those involved in the conflict are ready for a step-by-step solution to the conflict.

The most logical way of dealing positively with conflict is to use the basic **problem solving method** which has been used in business and science for many years. This basic problem solving technique is often referred to as the scientific method. The method leads to the solution of a conflict through answering five questions: (1) What is the conflict? (2) What are the facts? (3) What is my overall objective? (4) What are some possible solutions? and (5) What is the best solution? This method of solving a conflict may also be very useful to you in decision-making. If you have a tough decision, answer the five questions. The answers will lead you to a sound decision.

What Is the Conflict? The first step in solving a conflict is to state it clearly. This is not always an easy task. You may know something is wrong—you are in conflict with another—but you don't know exactly what. It is often said that a conflict well stated is a conflict half solved. How should you state the conflict? One way is to ask a question. Care must be taken, however, not to give judgments in the statement of the conflict. Be objective; do not favor anyone. Just state the conflict in specific terms.

For example, assume that you have been working in a shipping and receiving department for two years. The supervisor, John Phillips, suddenly retires because of ill health. You are promoted to his position over the head of Joan Tyler, a veteran of the company and the person who expected to be made supervisor. Joan is polite to you but uncooperative. She does her job and that's all. Worse still, the other twenty-three workers in the division are beginning to take sides. How would you state this problem? It is *not*: Why should Joan Tyler act like this? It is *not*: Should a person be promoted over the heads of those who have been in the firm longer? The problem is what you should do about the situation as it is. It could, of course, be stated in more than one way, but one possibility is the following: What steps can I take to improve the morale and production of this shipping and receiving department in light of the resentment felt over a newcomer's being made supervisor? You will notice that there is no question of right or wrong in this statement of the problem. Nor is there any attempt at a solution, which should be the last of the steps and not the first. This statement is also objective, another necessary feature.

What Are the Facts?   When you answer the second question, "What are the facts?," you must be careful to write down only facts, not opinions or value judgments. The facts must relate specifically to the problem. You must keep out all prejudice, all "oughts" and "shoulds." For instance, it is not a fact if you say Joan Tyler is acting like a spoiled child. A statement of this kind implies a judgment of the facts rather than a statement of them. An objective statement of the same implication would be that Joan Tyler does not cooperate to the extent she did before the promotion. The facts, then, should be stated without emotional coloring.

After you have stated as many real facts as you can that apply to the problem you wish to solve, it will be helpful if you will arrange them so that the most important facts—the ones that make a difference in the solution—are at the head of your list.

What Is My Overall Objective?   The third step is the hardest one. Perhaps you have never really thought about your main goal in a particular situation. It really helps, though, if you can force yourself to write down exactly where you want to go, exactly where you are headed.

In the shipping and receiving department problem, for example, your overall objective may be to keep your job. You don't want to be fired. Or your overall objective may be broader. You want to keep your job, bring peace to the department, and place departmental productivity at an even higher level than it was before your promotion. You don't want to resign in favor of Joan Tyler just to have peace restored. By now you can see that thinking the question through logically will help you to decide what your real objective is.

What Are Some Possible Solutions? The fourth step is to write down as many solutions to your conflict you can think of. One method of clearing the way for a good solution is to write down the extreme solutions first. Extreme solutions are seldom the best ones. In our conflict, such solutions would be: (1) Fire Joan Tyler. (2) Resign from your job as supervisor. (3) Resign from the company. Now the way is clear to devote your attention to constructive solutions—those which would take into consideration the complex human relation factors involved yet would be forward-looking in terms of getting the work of the division done well.

What Is the Best Solution? The last step is to choose the best solution. The best solution will meet the two parts of the following standard: (1) The most important facts that you discovered in the second step must have been taken care of. That is, the best solution must improve the situation as it stands as far as the important elements of the conflict are concerned. (2) It must help and not hinder you in reaching your overall objective.

In the situation under discussion, the best solution might have a number of parts. There would be first, the solution in terms of Joan Tyler,

ILLUSTRATION 9–3. It is a fact that in any kind of work, there must be some distance between the one in authority and the ones over whom such authority exists.

the resentful employee. It might be well to ignore her negative attitude and begin to build a better feeling between the two of you. This could begin by asking her (without making too much of it) to take charge of some project. This could be followed by commendation for any good work that she does. The best solution for you, as a new, inexperienced supervisor, would be to give yourself time to grow into the job. In any kind of work, authority cannot be maintained on a equality basis. In other words, there must be some distance between the one in authority and the ones over whom such authority exists. You must not expect to be liked by all of the workers under you. Because you have been chosen by your superiors to do a job, however, you should do all you can to make that job a success. An impersonal attitude toward negative feelings of others, plus a sincere determination to merit your workers' respect, will go a long way toward bringing about the needed change in their attitudes. If you keep your attention on getting the work done, while you are fair and positive toward those who work under you, you should expect the morale of the division to improve in time.

You are now armed with your third weapon for becoming a person who makes things happen. With the five-step decision-making method, you are equipped to solve the conflicts that come up in every possible line of work—as well as the problems that come up in your personal life. One reason for the success of the five-step method is the mental attitude you must adopt if you are to follow the first three steps. You cannot answer the first three questions (What is the conflict? What are the facts? and What is my overall objective?) until you become detached emotionally from the situation. When you can shelve your emotions temporarily and put your mature self in charge, you may find that the correct decision appears to you before you get to step four. The secret of good decision-making is to use mental judgment rather than the emotional pitfalls of "getting even" or "showing who is in charge." Practice in making decisions by the five-step method is one of the best-known ways of putting your self in charge.

QUESTIONS AND PROJECTS

1. What behaviors do you indulge in during conflict that make solutions more difficult?

2. Identify whether the following conflicts are examples of simple conflict conflict (fc), ego conflict (ec), or value conflict (vc).

_____ Harriet tells her coworker, ''Pick up your mess—I'm not your servant!'' The coworker replies, ''I thought we had agreed that it's your job to straighten the office. I take care of maintaining the equipment.''

_____ Dean believes that since he is regarded as an excellent archer, Wes should not question his archery form.

_____ Peg defends her failure to present a birthday gift to Adam by insisting that his birthday is not today (January 12) but January 22.

_____ Jack wants to start a vegetarian diet, but his roommate Sam insists that everyone needs the protein which is provided by meat.

_____ Frank says that if you quit a job it is your problem. Evelyn insists that everyone should be entitled to unemployment compensation.

3. Describe an ego conflict or value conflict in which you have been involved. How was the conflict resolved? Has it been resolved?

4. Discuss why ego conflict is so difficult to resolve.

5. Describe a human relations conflict that exists among your friends or work group. Go through the five steps given in this chapter, from stating the problem to choosing the best solution. Try to be completely objective. Submit your conflict and the steps to solving it for evaluation.

6. Why is it so important to have the proper attitudes before entering into the conflict-solving steps?

7. Describe a human relations problem that exists among those of your acquaintance. Go through the five steps given in this chapter, from stating the problem to choosing the best solution. Try to be completely objective. Submit your problem for evaluation.

8. In order to get along with all sorts of customers, you will need intelligence and tact. What would you say:

   a. To an angry customer who says, ''I thought you said this material was silk. It's marked synthetic blend.'' (You made a careless error in stating facts.)

   b. To a trying customer who says, ''Why do I have to buy the whole unit? All I need is this one part.''

   c. To a customer who runs a large account who says, ''I placed this order a month ago. Either fill it or forget it!''

9. The following situations are presented for your decision as to how you

would handle them. Write your exact words and the probable replies of the other person.

a. Your supervisor, Mr. Montesari, is away for a week on business. One of the managers comes in and demands that you call him long distance because of a personal conflict with another manager. You have Mr. Montesari's itinerary, but he asked you not to bother him with ordinary matters, since he plans to be very busy and seldom in one place long enough to take a telephone call. Ms. Nakamura, the assistant to Mr. Montesari, is handling routine matters.

b. An important sales representative, James Metzner, whose products are used by your company, comes in and asks to see Mr. Montesari.

c. Mr. Montesari returns from his business trip. The morning has been hectic. He has a board of directors' meeting at 10:30. It is now 10:25. He says, "Are those reports ready? Where are the tables I gave you to type? Where did I put those statements? Did you call Karen Olsen, the electrician?" You have taken care of all these details. How will you answer Mr. Montesari?

d. At noon, just before going to lunch, Mr. Montesari returns from his board of directors' meeting in a bad mood. He says, "Where in thunder did you put that letter from Washington? I had it in my briefcase, but it isn't there now! Can't I keep anything around here without somebody running off with it?" Mr. Montesari had asked you to file the letter just after he came in that morning. What do you do or say?

e. At 3:30 Mr. Montesari is meeting in his office with the two vice presidents on a serious matter. He told you as he went in to the meeting that he was not to be disturbed. An important client comes in on urgent business, something that cannot wait. What do you do or say?

CASE PROBLEMS

1. Identifying Conflict.

Linda Jacobi started working for a local bakery shop as an assistant. She understood that she would be helping the owner, Arthur O'Neill, with the baking process. Linda has been working for six months and has not assisted Mr. O'Neill with any baking. She is still doing routine tasks such as ordering supplies, cleaning the display racks, and store cleaning. Linda thinks her talents are being wasted, as she has had some training as a baker. She has asked Mr. O'Neill about helping with baking, but each time he replies, "We'll get to that later.'' He does intend to let Linda work with the process, but business has been very good and O'Neill feels he can do the work more quickly himself. Linda feels discouraged and disappointed in her job. She begins to dread going to work and has a difficult time controlling her anger and disappointment. Linda has decided that today she will tell O'Neill that if she is not allowed to help with the baking she will quit.

    a.   What is the major conflict in this situation?

    b.   Who or what is responsible for this conflict?

    c.   What are Linda's needs? Mr. O'Neill's needs?

    d.   What could Mr. O'Neill do to settle this conflict?

    e.   If you were Mr. O'Neill, how would you react to Linda's threat to quit?

    f.   What steps would you recommend to solve this conflict?

2. In the Groove.

Isabella Rodriguez, who has been transferred from the main office to one of its branches, finds it difficult to adapt to the new branch office methods. She continually refers to her old position: ''Miss McHenry wanted all computer print-outs set up this way,'' is one of her pet sayings. Some of Isabella's ideas are good, and in time she may be able to contribute to the efficiency of the branch office routines. At present, however, she annoys her coworkers. Unless Isabella adjusts to the new situation and accepts the branch policies, she is in danger of losing her job.

    a.   What conflicts may Isabella be setting herself up for with her present attitude?

    b.   What should Isabella's attitude be toward her job?

    c.   Why is it best for a newcomer to refrain from making suggestions about changes?

    d.   If Isabella's ideas are good, how and when may she present them for consideration?

3. Who's in Charge?

Lennie Owen had been working for three weeks as an office manager for McReynolds Brothers. Lennie is a highly competent worker, yet he felt lucky to get the job with McReynolds Brothers since many of the companies he applied to were hesitant to hire a man as an office worker. Lennie gets along well with the boss, Harry McReynolds, and most of his coworkers. The exception is Alice Jackson. Alice is snoopy and is constantly looking over Lennie's shoulder. Alice is also extremely bossy. She is often so busy making suggestions to others that she does not get her own work done.

Lennie doesn't like being ordered around by Alice. Trying to work with her is very difficult. The problem is that Alice has worked for McReynolds Brothers for fifteen years and is a good friend of the owners. Lennie likes his job and needs the money.

Lennie has special plans for the evening. Ordinarily he is most willing to work a few minutes late, but he is anxious to get home on time tonight. Alice has let her work fall behind and orders Lennie to help out. Lennie realizes that he will be an hour late if he helps complete her work. He would really like to tell Alice off and leave her stuck, but he is afraid he would be risking his job.

    a.   Do you recommend that Lennie stay and help with Alice's work?

    b.   What is the real conflict in this case study?

    c.   How would you describe Alice's behavior? Why do you think Alice acts the way she does?

    d.   What are some ways in which this conflict could be worked out?

4. No Laughing Matter.

Abby Bergman has a reputation in the store as a practical joker. She has pulled every gag in the book. Many of Abby's coworkers think her tricks are funny and that she livens up the workplace. Abby likes being known and recognized as the store's joker. She enjoys the extra attention. Several of her coworkers, however, feel that she wastes time and creates more work for others. They find her antics childish and immature. Emily has tried to ignore Abby's jokes, as she has trouble controlling her temper.

Today, Abby moved Emily's chair from its usual position; this caused Emily to fall as she attempted to sit. Emily hurt her wrist, bumped her head, and suffered from embarrassment. She became very angry, lost her temper, and swore at Abby. She warned Abby never to come near her again.

    a.   What is the conflict in this case?

    b.   Is the conflict one that will soon solve itself?

    c.   What are Abby's special needs?

    d.   How do you think Abby feels about the accident?

    e.   What would you do if you were Emily? How would you greet Abby the day following the accident?

    f.   How can this conflict be resolved?

5. The Difficult Boss.

Miss Tims, a patent attorney, is struggling to build up her own business. To save money, she hires young and inexperienced office workers. She is demanding and criticizes her employees angrily when they make any mistakes. She constantly reminds them how much work there is to be done and tells them they should work faster. An example of a daily occurrence follows:

Charles, a conscientious beginner, presents a letter to Miss Tims for her signature in which he has added an undictated comma; the rules of punctuation demanded the change. When Miss Tims notices this one change in an otherwise perfect letter, she calls Charles to her desk, crosses out the comma, and writes "Retype" in pen across the top of the page. Charles is upset; now he will have to retype the letter when he could have erased the offending comma. Moreover, he feels he was right in his action.

Anne, who is dependable and efficient, has spent several minutes trying to find the correct spelling of a peculiar name in the telephone directory. She finally turns to Charles to see if he has any idea of how to spell it. Before Charles has a chance to reply, Miss Tims (who has her desk in the same room) looks up and says, "Work on your own projects, people."

Both Charles and Anne find the work interesting, but they feel the only solution to the problem is to resign.

Solve the problem with the five-step method described in Chapter 9.

6.   Is the Customer Always Right?

An irate customer enters a plumbing supply store with a faucet that she has purchased from a salesperson who said the faucet would fit her bathroom sink. The customer has obviously installed the faucet incorrectly, thereby ruining the gaskets and scratching the chrome finish. The customer proceeds to vent all her anger on Chris Gallegos, who is taking the regular salesperson's place that day.

    a.   Is this situation a common happening?

    b.   If you were Chris, what would you say to the customer? Would you try to handle the situation yourself? Why or why not?

    c.   Was the customer justified in the complaint?

    d.   If you had been the customer, how would you have handled the situation?

10

Managing Stress and Emotions

LEARNING OBJECTIVES:

1. Define the concept and causes of stress.
2. Explain the signals of stress.
3. Explain the various methods of dealing with stress.
4. Understand the concept of emotional temperature.
5. Explain the techniques of managing your emotions.

Derek's work no longer gives him satisfaction or a feeling of self-worth. His hobbies, recreational activities, and social life mean little to him. Coworkers annoy him, noise in the office bothers him, and no one can please him. He finds himself snapping at his boss, lashing out at coworkers, ignoring friends, brooding in frustration, and feeling "down" most of the time. He prefers to be alone and doing nothing. Derek is beginning to see his friends pull away. He has picked up clues that his coworkers and superiors are not supporting him for a promotion for which he is qualified. Finally, Derek begins to take a serious look at what was happening to his life. He starts by asking himself, "What is wrong with me?" and "How can I turn my life around?"

____*One* of the difficulties encountered in growing on the job is that of becoming a whole person—in other words, getting yourself together. In fact, no big step should ever be taken when you feel torn, splintered, or not all together. The ideal state, of course, would be to go through life "in one solid piece." However, the everyday stresses of living this ideal state don't allow you to always remain "one solid piece." Before you can begin to grow, you must get yourself together, find out what you are, and know what you think and feel. In short, you must become and feel like a real person—not just somebody's employee, daughter, son, wife, husband, or whatever.

To be able to feel deeply the good things of life is a real blessing. Positive emotions make our lives worth living. But what about the negative emotions and stressful feelings of everyday life. What do they do to us? When you are seized by anger, confusion, jealousy, fear, worry, or doubt, can you handle your usual tasks with efficiency and skill? The destructive emotions and stressful situations are just that. They destroy peace of mind, well-being, and cause you to feel that you're not in control of your job and your life.

WHAT IS STRESS?

The code word in our society for feeling out of control and letting others know that you are hurting psychologically and not feeling whole is **stress**. Stress is anything that causes physical or mental tension. Stress is a pressure from your surroundings that causes an imbalance or a disturbance in your life. Stress in our society is often self-caused: stress to achieve, stress to complete, stress to compete, stress to accomplish, stress to manage the confusion in everyday events, stress to pass a test, or stress to excel.

Where does stress come from? What really causes stress? These are difficult questions because stress is an individual thing. What causes stress for you may not bother someone else. Most experts agree that the single most important cause of stress is *change*. This is especially true when changes come too rapidly or too many upheavals arrive in a person's life at the same time. For example, Sue Ellen has just completed a program in fashion merchandising. She is anxious to get started on her new job. Her mother is ill and requires an extreme amount of care. Her father died a few months ago. Sue Ellen's new job requires that she be relocated in a town one hundred miles from home. The move, a new career, and a change in family relationships may cause excessive stress for her. Too many changes have arrived at the same time.

You may need to monitor your life and guard against allowing too many changes to take place at one time.

Other stress causes related to the work world include: adjustment to a new job, conditions and requirements of work, performance evaluations, characteristics of coworkers or supervisors, job discrimination, recognition relating to job performance, or even resistance to change. Common stressful circumstances of daily living may include: separation from loved ones, economic difficulties, fatigue, loss of self-esteem, illness, illness of a loved one, a life-style not consistent with your upbringing, or continued conflicts with friends or relatives.

Stress is not a total villain. Stress is not always unpleasant and is not always caused by something unpleasant. Winning a million dollars can be stressful. Stress helps us remain alert and ready to tackle problems. Only when stress is excessive and creates emotional or physical problems does it rob you of long-term productivity and a sense of feeling whole. Thus, the key to keeping yourself on an even keel is the ability to manage the stress which is unavoidable in your life. Even though the causes of too much stress are often beyond your control, you can learn to contain stress so that it works for and not against you.

If stress is not a total villain, perhaps it would be good to take a look at when stress should be of concern to you. You need to be able to identify the difference between normal, everyday stress and serious and damaging stress that can lead to a lack of productivity or even a physical or mental breakdown.

STRESS SIGNALS

Some danger signs of damaging stress to be concerned about follow:

1. Physical feelings which you are not accustomed to experiencing. Physical feelings are generally one of the first signs of too much stress. The physical warning signals usually listed by medical experts as signs of harmful stress may include: pounding of the heart, a dryness of the throat or mouth, insomnia, feeling constantly tired, inability to concentrate on any one thing, chronic pain in the neck or lower back, stomach pain, decreased or increased appetite, nightmares, an overpowering urge to cry or escape, difficulty in breathing, or trembling. Often we ignore these stress signs as they seem to come and go. If these feelings are totally disregarded, more serious conditions may develop.

2. Sudden changes in mood or character. If you are under a great

ILLUSTRATION 10-1.   Insomnia is one of the physical warning signals of harmful
              stress.

deal of stress, your behavior may become unpredictable. You may do things that are not a usual part of your personality or typical behavior. If you explode or express extreme disgust with others or yourself and this is unexplainable, you may be experiencing too much stress. If you are uncomfortable with a new position or additional responsibilities, you may experience a change of character brought on by too much stress. Unfortunately, you may be unaware of the changes in your mood or behavior. The changes may have to be pointed out to you by others.

3. Depression. **Depression** is an emotional disorder which is marked by sadness, inactivity, and a feeling of emptiness. Depressions may be caused by too much stress. Depression at its maximum may cause an overstressed person to withdraw from coworkers, family, and friends. The depressed person may begin to feel emotionally drained, sick, or numb. If you are experiencing depression, you may lose interest in your work, family, friends, and hobbies.

If you are experiencing many changes in your life, or if things haven't been going well for you, it would be good to give some thought to the above three signs of stress in search of answers.

DEALING WITH STRESS

The good news about stress is that you often cause it; therefore, you can also prevent or decrease most of your stress. The following hints may be helpful to you if you feel certain that stress is being experienced.

Deal with the cause. If tension and stress come from your relationship with a person, talk out your differences. The longer you try to contain yourself, the more stress you will build up. If tension comes because you have put off an unfinished task, restructure your priorities so you can get the task you have been avoiding out of the way and off your mind.

Develop techniques to deal with the causes of stress. Write down the problems you are having with relationships on a piece of paper. Make it a point to call or face the person causing a stress in your life and talk out your differences. Take the tasks that you have been procrastinating on completing, write them down, and check them off as you take care of them. You may find yourself avoiding the causes of stress by simply saying, "I am not feeling well," "I'm just tired," or by taking your frustration and stress out on others with unkind thoughts, words, or actions. Avoid this type of behavior and deal with the reality of the situation.

Work at pacing yourself. It is only natural to want to be an achiever. In your struggle to be an achiever, you may put yourself in high gear for long periods of time. These long periods may prove to be too much for your emotional and physical health. Stop and "smell the roses." As you are working toward a goal, you reach points where it is appropriate to stop and reward yourself for a job well done. This reward period will allow you to relax and get away from the pressure. For example, Robert recently started working as a grocery checkout clerk. He has set for himself a goal of being an assistant manager within a period of three years. He works extremely hard at his job and strives to learn everything he can by observing others and asking questions about the grocery business. After one year, Robert is promoted to assistant produce manager. He is thrilled. In his anxiousness to continue to climb toward his goal, he puts in voluntary overtime, helps everyone in his department, and provides special services for preferred customers. He ignores the fact that he has built up vacation time. Some nights he is unable to sleep because he is thinking about some phase of his new position. He loses weight and frequently feels tense. Robert needs to learn to pace himself. It would have been wise for him to take a few of his earned vacation days as a reward period and celebrate his success soon after he was comfortable in the new position.

Strive for flexibility and accept some imperfection. Take it easy on yourself. It is impossible to pay attention to all areas of your life at the same time. Take care of things as you can. Do not expect perfection of yourself or others. Realize there are some things that you cannot control. Learn to accept what you cannot change or alter.

Lois and Arthur started working as desk clerks in a hotel in their community on the same day. Lois wants very much to please the management staff and has clear goals in mind. Lois works very hard to accommodate customers. She answers the phone courteously, goes out of her way to get along with everyone, and follows company policies relating to procedures and hospitality. Arthur is often indifferent to guests, ignores special guest requests, and frequently violates company policies by taking shortcuts. Arthur's attitude bothers Lois, and she cannot overlook his shortcomings. She tries to cover for him by doing some of his work as well as her own. She makes tactful suggestions to him whenever possible about his attitude, and she worries about his job performance. She cannot accept the imperfections she has identified in Arthur's work. These imperfections eventually cause her so much stress that she loses her enthusiasm for the position and the goal which she has set for herself. Lois finds herself dreading the thought of going to work. She even considers forgetting about a career in the hotel industry. She is generally miserable. Lois has not learned to accept what she cannot change or alter.

You cannot change the work habits of others. You cannot always be responsible for the actions of others. Try not to let a similar situation happen to you. Do what you can to help others, but don't expect others to have the same values and standards which you have established for yourself.

Ask yourself if you are aiming at the unreasonable or the impossible. If you are trying to live up to someone else's expectations or expecting others to live up to your standards, you may be spinning your wheels. List your talents and weaknesses and find a pattern for your life that is comfortable for you. Remember, you are only human—imperfections are acceptable.

Talk out your troubles. Learn to talk things over with someone with whom you feel comfortable and trust. The talk will release pressure, make you feel better, and often someone else will help you see a new side of a problem. If you find yourself preoccupied with a difficulty, don't let it get you down. Turn to a good listener and discuss what is troubling you. In the process of describing your perceived problem, you may find an answer.

Manage your time well. Good time management can eliminate stress. Strive to work as efficiently as you can and continually seek ways of streamlining your work. Work to complete tasks on time and in an expedient manner. Attempt to break down big jobs into reasonable blocks of work. This is a good way to tackle what seems like an overwhelming task and to feel rewarded as you complete each step. Delegate and share work with others when appropriate and acceptable. Avoid attempting to do everything yourself. Keep your workload under control and reasonable.

Look at the bright side. Attempt to develop a positive outlook on life. Always strive to concentrate on what is positive. Look beyond yourself, and avoid spending too much time thinking about failure. There have been studies which prove that positive feelings help fight disease, while negative ones can produce or intensify illness.

Whenever the opportunity arises, try to turn negative statements made by others into positive ones. If a coworker says, "We will never get this report done," respond, "If we work together, I think we can do it!" A positive thought will introduce a new spirit and get everyone working hard to achieve. A positive spirit will indeed help reduce stress levels.

Participate in physical exercise. Exercise can help to relieve stress. An effective exercise program can "burn up" the physical tension that builds up in your body during a long period of stress. Activity such as moderate walking can relieve tension and relax your body. Other good forms of physical release from stress are playing tennis, running, bicycling, or other forms of exercise which you enjoy. If you have had a stressful morning, skip the coffee break and try a walk break. A brisk walk through corridors or around the block may bring to you a brighter outlook.

Diet. Diet can play an important role in dealing with excessive amounts of stress. Most medical experts agree that cutting down on fatty meats, dairy

ILLUSTRATION 10–2.
A greater consumption of fruits, vegetables, and grains have a calming effect on a stressed person.

products, eggs, sweets, and salt will relieve stress. It is generally recommended that a greater consumption of fruits, vegetables, poultry, fish, and whole grains have a calming effect on a stressed person.

Get involved in a wellness program. Employers across the country are realizing that stress may be an important factor in employee productivity. Companies realize that stress can contribute to absenteeism and alcohol and drug abuse and harm good human relationships. Many companies have started wellness programs or joined a local health agency's program. Participation in a wellness program can help you counteract the effects of too much stress before it becomes harmful to you.

Take Your Emotional Temperature

No matter how you have felt about your personality in the past, the important point is how you are doing right now. The trouble with many improvement campaigns is that they go the wrong way. We measure the mistakes we have made, how we have failed. A much more fruitful exercise is to measure how we have succeeded. Furthermore, your personality growth is an individual matter. It won't help you if you pattern your personal qualities after those of someone else. What you need instead is some kind of standard, some indication of your own personal growth.

Fourteen of Maslow's[1] points make up a description of a person who is all together, who is OK, and who feels OK. Maslow calls such a person a self-actualizing person. These fourteen points might be considered your emotional thermometer against which you can measure how you are doing from time to time. Remember, though, that there is no end to personal growth. We will never be totally free from personal faults. Still, it will help if we can see measurable improvement over the years. Measure yourself against these standards today; then go through the fourteen points again in six months. See if you have made any progress.

1. You will be able to detect the fake, the phony, and the dishonest and to judge people correctly and efficiently. You will be able to perceive reality and be comfortable with reality. You will not be frightened by the unknown.
2. You will be able to accept. You will be able to accept yourself, accept others, accept nature without thinking about it much one

---

1. A. H. Maslow, *Motivation and Personality* (New York: Harper and Row, 1970), pp. 153-180.

way or another. You will enjoy your physical side without guilt. You will be able to be yourself and you will dislike artificiality in others. What you will feel guilty about are shortcomings that could be improved: laziness, hurting others, prejudice.

3. You will be spontaneous, simple, and natural. Your codes of behavior may be strict, but they will be your own.

4. You will be problem-centered; you won't fight the problem to defend your own ego. You won't spend time worrying about yourself but will do what needs to be done. You will be concerned with the good of people in general, and with all of the members of their families in general. You will seem to be above the small things of life. This will make life easier not only for you, but also for all who associate with you.

5. You will need detachment and privacy. You will like to be alone more than the average person does. You will be able to take personal misfortunes without reacting as the ordinary person does, violently.

6. You will become independent of your environment. Less healthy individuals must have people around them; but the self-actualizing person, the person who is concerned with personal growth, may be hampered by the clinging demands of others.

7. You will have the capacity to appreciate freshly, again and again, the basic goods in life. Any sunset is as beautiful as your first sunset; any flower is of breathtaking loveliness even after you have seen a million flowers. You will derive ecstasy, inspiration, and strength from the basic experiences of life—not from going to a nightclub, or getting a lot of money, or having a good time at a party.

8. The mystic experience may be fairly common to you. You may experience the feeling of being simultaneously more powerful and more helpless than you ever were before, of great wonder and awe, of the loss of place in time.

9. You will have a deep sympathy and affection for human beings in general.

10. You will have a few very close friends.

11. You will have an unhostile sense of humor. The kind of jokes Abraham Lincoln told—mainly about himself—will be the type you like.

12. You will be creative, original, and inventive. This does not mean a special creativeness, but rather that you will be creative within

the scope of your own natural talents. You will find joy in a new approach to your task.

13. You may not always be a conformist. You will get along with the culture in various ways; but while you will not be rebellious in the adolescent sense, you will resist conformity.

14. You will make some mistakes. You will not be totally free from guilt, sadness, and conflict—because these conditions are normal in our lives today. But you will be able to accept your own blame, pick up the pieces, and go on.

Learn to Manage Your Emotions

In order to control any emotion that may be a problem to you—jealousy, worry, fear—you must first identify it, describe it, state what it is. You should do the same thing with a destructive emotion: Define the emotion. What is *worry*, for example? You might say that it is a nameless dread for which you can find no real cause.

The next step in your campaign to control destructive emotions is to write down what the emotion does, what its manifestations are. You might say that worry causes sleeplessness or, in some cases, sleeping too much; lack of appetite or overeating; headaches; mental blocks; lack of physical coordination; or a poor memory for facts that you know. Excessive and prolonged worrying may cause you to become depressed.

The third step is to give an example, in your own life or in the life of someone you know, of what the emotion has brought about. This serves as a dramatic object lesson, showing vividly why it is wise to learn to control this emotion. In the case of worry, there is hardly a student anywhere who has not had the experience of worrying over an examination to the point of not being able to think at all. This kind of experience shows the destructiveness of worry better than any number of abstract statements.

The fourth step is to write down all of the possible actions that might help to control the destructive emotion. In the case of worry, the list might include the following:

1. Set aside a certain time of day, or day of the week, for worrying. Then, when a worrisome thought enters your mind, just file it away to be worried about on Thursday!

2. Do something about the cause of the worry. If you worry about finances, start a budget. If you worry about failing a course in school, study an extra half-hour a day.

3. Invent some mental process that will automatically take place

whenever the tendency to give in to the emotion arises. In the case of anger, you might think of something beautiful—a lovely lake you have seen, the melody of a favorite musical selection, or a line from a favorite poem. In the case of worry, one of the best devices is a slogan. Some of these are old, but they are still around because they have proved their effectiveness through the generations. Such slogans as "Take one step at a time," "Rome was not built in a day," "What will it matter in a thousand years?" might help in the case of worry.

4. Forget the past. This is an important rule in the case of most of the destructive emotions. We get angry at a best friend and rake up old resentments from the past only to find we no longer have a best friend. It is almost impossible to hear someone rebuke us for a past action without retaliating in kind. Too often we speak words that cause wounds we can never heal. Whatever the emotion you are working on, forget your past failures. The past is gone; nothing can be done about it, so let it go.

5. Do or say something positive in line with the emotion. If you hate someone or dislike someone intensely, the best way to get rid of this emotion is to do something positive, something considerate, for that person. It is almost impossible to dislike someone for whom you have just done a kindness. The magic does not work, however, if you expect *any* kind of reward for your good deed. Don't expect to be thanked. The kindness should be done merely because it is good for *you* to do it. There will be intangible benefits, but don't look for a reward. In fact, the best way to accomplish this is to do something considerate anonymously; this is guaranteed to take the sting of hatred away from that person.

What Emotions Say to Us

Whatever our emotional difficulty—fear, anger, jealousy, hate, worry—there is a reason for its being there. Sometimes the reason is the exact opposite of what the emotion appears to be. It may be the other side of the coin. If you are jealous of someone's affection, for example, this may not mean that you care for the person deeply. It may mean instead that you are insecure about your own worth. You cannot believe that you are worthy of love; therefore, you cling possessively to the person who is closest to you. If you hate someone, this emotion says that you feel unappreciated. You are filled with resentment because your ability, accomplishment, or knowledge has not received recognition, while someone else's have. Then this person has had the nerve to belittle you in some way! It is the belittling that triggers the dislike, but the lack of appreciation is the real cause.

Envy is a powerful emotion, but here we are not sure of our abilities. Perhaps we would like to be brilliant or talented but feel we are not. The envious emotions say that we are insecure and that we resent this insecurity.

Worry, the kind that has no known cause, comes from hostility that we refuse to admit. That is why it is important that we take a good look at worry and at ourselves. We must admit that we are not perfect, that we may have negative feelings toward those we should love.

What We Should Say to Emotions

No matter what the emotion may be that is making your life miserable, you must not let it control you. Learn to control it. Listen to what it tells you; then do something to change the situation that brings the emotion about. This means that you should become more lovable instead of being jealous and possessive. It means that you should become more appreciative of the accomplishments of others. Sooner or later someone will, in return, become appreciative of your accomplishments.

Don't waste your life waiting for people to come to you. Take the first step. Then, while you are appreciating the achievements of others, work

ILLUSTRATION 10-3.
Choose an activity that gives you the most satisfaction and that you do reasonably well. Work hard to master it.

USDA Photo

hard to become an expert at one thing. Many of us try to be musicians, writers, actors, debaters, athletes, and political leaders all at once. No one can succeed in so many different fields. Choose the one activity that gives you the most satisfaction and that you do reasonably well. Then concentrate on that activity. Be willing to start at the bottom. Be willing to work on the team. It will not be long before your worth is recognized.

QUESTIONS AND PROJECTS

1. Prepare a list of stressful situations that come into your life from time to time. Opposite each stressful situation you list, write a suggestion to yourself to help eliminate it.

2. Think about the last time you had some time all to yourself, a time you had to share with no one else. Did you plan for that alone time? What did you think about during that alone time? Are you looking forward to the next period of alone time? What do you plan to do with that time the next time it occurs?

3. Think for a moment about an incident from your past, a moment when you were very unhappy with someone. Write a list of the reasons for your feelings of unhappiness. Be honest with yourself. Analyze for a moment the actions you took and the results of those actions. Write the highlights of a different plan of action that may have been more appropriate or less stressful for you and others.

4. Have you ever observed people who had been so stressed that they lost their tempers? If so, what was the result? Did you see any other way the people could have avoided losing their tempers? Why is it that we can often make helpful suggestions to others about controlling temper, but we have a difficult time in helping ourselves?

5. Schedule an interview with a health professional. Prepare a series of questions for that individual about the impact that stress can have on physical and emotional health and well-being.

6. Do you have any special tactics you use to control your emotions when you find yourself in a stressful situation? Does your body send out any warning signals when you are under stress? What are the signals? Do you pay attention to those signals?

7. Have you ever tried any of the techniques suggested in this chapter to help relieve stress? If you have, what were they? What were the

results? Do you know others who have tried these techniques? What successes did they experience? Why might some techniques work for you but not for others?

CASE PROBLEMS

1. Emotional Displays.

Suzanne feels like crying. She has been on her new job for one week. The assistant manager, Sheila Matthews, just spoke to her sharply because she spent half an hour showing clothes to a difficult customer who walked out without buying anything. Suzanne is putting the clothes back on the hangers, clearing the dressing room, and fighting hard to hold back the tears. Harold Simpson, a coworker, notices Suzanne and recalls how he felt the first time he was reprimanded. He tries to put together words that will help Suzanne to regain quickly her composure and self-esteem.

    a.   How might Harold help Suzanne get through these stressful moments?
    b.   Should Sheila Matthews speak to her sales personnel as she does?
    c.   Would it be wise for Harold to suggest to Suzanne that she ignore Sheila's remarks?
    d.   What constructive suggestions could Harold make to help Suzanne?

2. Overworked.

Lloyd has been in the position of assistant manager for a fast-food operation for two months. He supervises fifteen full-time employees and ten part-time workers. He does all the food and beverage ordering, takes care of promotional items and advertising, and opens and closes the restaurant every day. The cleaning crew is often late or does not show up at all, and Lloyd ends up cleaning the floor, equipment, and the restrooms. Lloyd finds himself snapping at dependable employees and faithful customers. He often feels tense, has an upset stomach, and has annoying headaches. Lloyd sees his family physician and is told that perhaps he is working too hard and too many hours. Lloyd doesn't see any alternatives. He continues to work as he has in the past.

    a.   What could possibly be the end result of Lloyd's situation?
    b.   Why do some people work themselves into situations similar to this?
    c.   Would you recommend that Lloyd give up the position? If not, what would you recommend that he do about his workload.
    d.   What additional information would you like to know about Lloyd?

3. Promotion Stress.

Willard Moser has been working for the Hartwell Association, a public rela-

PERSONALITY DEVELOPMENT FOR WORK

tions firm, for several years and has done a good job. In his performance evaluations, which are done every six months, there is only one negative comment that continues to surface—Willard puts too much nervous energy into ordinary tasks. He puts so much detail into routine work that when a high-pressure, more complex problem comes along, he gets very tense, works too fast, and in general his work falls below his usual standard. The personnel manager is looking for a private secretary for the director of the firm, Tom Tanaka. Tom wants a secretary with energy and initiative, who can take care of clients while he is away from the office. Tom travels a good deal. In looking over evaluations of people in the office who might be promoted to the private secretary position, Tom is impressed with Willard's credentials. His skills are good, and he has an associate degree from a two-year community college program. Tom interviews Willard and finds him to be the best candidate. Tom tells the personnel manager he wants Willard for the position. The personnel manager mentions Willard's problem, which has surfaced as the only criticism of his work. Tom informs personnel that he will want Willard to begin working for him in six weeks. The personnel manager is charged with correcting Willard's problem in this time period.

   a.   If you were the personnel manager, what would you do? (Refer to the problem solving method presented in Chapter 9 in answering this question.)
   b.   Do you feel that six weeks will be a long enough period of time to help Willard prepare for this new opportunity?
   c.   Would you suggest to Willard that he not accept this career move?
   d.   What may happen to Willard if he is unsuccessful in this new position?
   e.   Is it always wise to ''go for'' a new opportunity?

11

Recognizing Discrimination

LEARNING OBJECTIVES:

1. Understand the terms discrimination, prejudice, and stereotyping.

2. Explain the types of discrimination which are considered illegal.

3. Explain the damage discrimination can do in the workplace.

4. Illustrate strategies for dealing effectively with discrimination in the workplace.

> Mr. Aubrey, the high school custodian, needed help with the maintenance of the building after school hours. Judy and Tom were hired on the same day. The work they did was very similar. They cleaned restrooms, emptied wastebaskets, swept hallways, washed windows, and did minor repair work on the building. One evening while Judy and Tom were taking a break, Tom mentioned to Mr. Aubrey that he wanted to leave an hour early on Friday evening to get an early start on the road for a weekend of fishing. Mr. Aubrey said, ''Sure, take off and have a good time.'' Judy overheard the conversation and was somewhat upset as she had asked to come in an hour late one evening so that she could attend her child's school program. Mr. Aubrey denied her request. He had said to her, ''I'm

> sorry, but you were hired to work from seven to eleven p.m.
> and I expect you to be here." Tom and Judy were talking one
> evening about the cost of living. Tom mentioned that he was
> thinking about asking Mr. Aubrey to recommend him for a
> raise. In the course of the conversation, Judy discovered that
> Tom was making twenty-five cents more per hour than she
> was. Judy was a victim of unfair treatment—discrimination.

___ **"That's** not fair!" Have you ever found yourself in a situation where these words came into your mind—or your mouth? We all have an inner sense of fairness, and when it is violated, we feel uncomfortable or angry. **Discrimination** is a word that is used to describe unfair treatment of a particular person due to race, sex, religious affiliation, or handicap. Discrimination is a behavior which is often based on an attitude. If you, as an individual, think that a particular race of people tend to be lazy, that is an attitude. If you were an employer and refused to hire people of that race, you would be guilty of discrimination.

PREJUDICE AND STEREOTYPING

Two other terms associated with discrimination are prejudice and stereotyping. **Prejudice** means to prejudge. An opinion is formed without taking the time or trouble to judge in a fair manner. Prejudice leads to treating a person unfairly. If you have decided that people belonging to a particular minority race are stupid, incompetent, and lazy, you will likely prejudge all people you meet belonging to that race. If you meet Ralph, a member of that minority group, you will prejudge him based on the inborn trait of being a member of that minority. You will be guilty of prejudging Ralph and all other members of the race. During our lives we often judge people on traits over which they have no control—race, sex, ethnic background, or physical features. We are also guilty of judging others on the basis of their environment—education, occupation, habits, lifestyle, or customs.

Whenever you judge others based on widely held beliefs about various groups rather than as unique individuals, you are guilty of **stereotyping**. If you stereotype an individual, you "pigeonhole" or categorize that person.

You assign that person a set of characteristics which may be unfair and undeserved. Stereotyping can also work in reverse. You may give people an unfair advantage by assigning them very positive traits because of the "pigeonhole" you have placed them in. For example, you may choose Alice as a friend based on where she went to school and the employment she now has. If you take a look at Alice as an individual, you may find that she has little in common with you and that her values are not in tune with yours. In this situation you have given Alice a more than fair advantage because of stereotyping. You have given her the privilege of being your friend, when perhaps she does not deserve it. Stereotyping is not only unfair; stereotypes are extremely likely to be inaccurate. That one person or five overweight persons are lazy does not mean that all overweight persons are lazy. Even if 95 percent of all overweight people are lazy, that does not mean that Beth, an overweight woman, is lazy. Stereotyping is very hard to fight because you can always find in a group one or more members with the characteristics that started the stereotype.

Discrimination, prejudice, and stereotyping are so much a part of our lives that we may hardly notice them. All too often our prejudices feel comfortable. We do not think about them. We may even endure the discomforts of prejudice against us in order to keep a job. Today, however, there is an effort to make people conscious of their prejudices and the damage which can be done by those feelings. Laws prohibit discriminatory practices on the basis of race, sex, religion, national origin, or physical or emotional handicaps.

In the case of Judy, Tom, and Mr. Aubrey, all three persons involved were at fault. Mr. Aubrey discriminated against Judy by treating her unfairly. He probably did not consider himself to be prejudiced, but he didn't take the time to consider her feelings and needs as he did for Tom. Judy was at fault for accepting the unfair treatment. She should have been aware of the discrimination and taken appropriate action to remedy it. Tom was at fault for accepting the advantages he was receiving. The first step in coping with discrimination in employment situations is to become aware of it. When prejudice becomes a part of your personality as a worker or when you learn to accept unfair treatment based on prejudice, a type of decay sets it. Work becomes less satisfying. Conflict becomes a part of each day of work. Often, your productivity will decrease. In order to be a better worker, you should work to remove these barriers to productivity and job satisfaction. You need to learn to recognize and not accept discrimination in the workplace. You must be sensitive to what is going on around you and must recognize your personal prejudices in order to change them. Prejudice and stereotyping are very difficult to overcome.

WHAT THE LAW PROVIDES

The Civil Rights Act became law in 1964. The strongest federal legislation in the area of job discrimination ever passed was the 1972 amendment to that legislation, Title VII. According to this Act, employers are not allowed to discriminate in any area of employment. Employers cannot discriminate in recruiting, hiring, promoting, discharging, classifying, or training employees. The agency responsible for enforcement of Title VII is the Equal Employment Opportunity Commission (EEOC). The EEOC receives and evaluates complaints either by trying to work out the problem or referring the complaint to the courts. This agency also develops guidelines to help organizations write and put into practice affirmative action programs.

Affirmative action is designed to correct the effect of past discrimination against minorities and women. Under affirmative action plans, employers list the discriminatory barriers in their organization that are limiting to minority applicants and current employees. Then plans are set up to eliminate those barriers. Affirmative action programs are required for organizations that receive federal funds or contract with the federal government, public, employers, and all federal agencies.

Race, Color, and National Origin

In the process of recruiting, selecting, and hiring workers, employers are prohibited from asking certain questions concerning race, color, or ethnic background. These questions are prohibited by law. The law makes it very clear that your race, color, or ethnic background should not be determining factors in whether you will be hired. Any employer may ask whether the applicant is a citizen of the United States. Questions regarding an individual's ability to speak or read a foreign language are also permitted. However, questions regarding ancestry or native language are not allowed. Such questions as, "What language did you speak at home as a child?" are illegal.

Religion

Gwen applied for a job as a retail clerk with a local department store. Based on the area of town Gwen lived in, the personnel officer, Gladys, determined that Gwen must be a Seventh-Day Adventist. Gladys gave Gwen no further consideration because the store was open on Saturday. Gladys knew that Adventists observed Saturday as their day of worship. This type of discrimination is not fair and obviously not legal. Over the past few decades, much of the discrimination against certain religions has

ILLUSTRATION 11-1.
Title VII insures that
employers cannot dis-
criminate in recruiting,
hiring, promoting, dis-
charging, classifying, or
training employees.

diminished, although it has not completely disappeared, as in the unfortunate case of Gwen.

As a job applicant, you should be advised concerning normal hours or days of work required by the employer. An employer may ask if you are willing to work the required schedule. An employer may not, however, quiz you about your religious denomination, religious practices, religious affiliations, or religious holidays.

Sex and Family Status

The language of Title VII indicates that you cannot be discriminated against because of your sex. This type of discrimination has been and continues to be a major issue in our society. As the traditional role of women has changed, more and more women are entering the work force to provide for the family income. Men, too, have taken a look at the roles assigned to them and are discovering that they have additional options. These redefined roles have caused some concern on the part of employers. Employers are concerned about: How much time will family obligations take? How often will the employee be absent for family commitments? How much time will be required away from the workplace if a new baby becomes a part of the family? Who is responsible for child care in the home?

ILLUSTRATION 11-2.
As the traditional role
of women changes, more
women enter the work
force to provide for the
family income.

The rules of fairness also apply in asking questions about family status. An employer may not ask your marital status. You do not need to provide information about whether you are single, engaged, married, divorced, or separated. Questions regarding the number and ages of children or plans for pregnancy are not legal. As an applicant, you may be asked if it will be possible to meet specific work schedules or if there are any activities, commitments, or responsibilities that may hinder you in meeting work attendance requirements. Other questions which may allow the employer to learn about your family status (without directly asking) can relate to expected duration on the job or anticipated absences. These questions may only be asked if they are asked of all applicants and weighed equally in evaluations for both sexes.

Handicaps

People with physical or mental handicaps may have found it difficult to get into the job market, even though the law protects their right to employment. However, those employers who have given the handicapped or challenged an opportunity have often found them to be excellent employees. Physical or mental handicaps may affect a person's ability to perform certain tasks. An employer, therefore, has a right to know about any handicap that may affect performance on a job. Inquiries may be made as to whether an applicant has a mental or physical handicap which should be considered in job placement. General questions that address handicaps or health conditions which do not directly relate to the job performance are not allowed.

Age

Ageism, as this form of discrimination can be called, can apply to the older worker (forty to seventy) and the younger worker (eighteen to thirty-five). Younger workers are often hired because they are less expensive and are stereotyped as more flexible and willing to learn. Younger workers can also be placed at a disadvantage because they have little experience. Older workers may be hired because of their experience, knowledge, and maturity. However, they may be discriminated against because their understanding of methods and technology may be considered dated. By law, in most situations, it is illegal to discriminate against an older or younger person during the hiring process. While employers may require a work permit (issued by school authorities) providing proof of age, an employer may not require a birth certificate as proof of age before hiring.

Character

Traditionally there is discrimination and prejudice in the workplace against those whose character does not meet with the general standards of society. Criminals, members of subversive organizations, those who are poor credit risks, and others who are considered to be "undesirables" are often not allowed to work even though their abilities to perform in a given occupation are not impaired by the low esteem our society gives them. In many cases, however, the law requires that such individuals should have equal opportunity in employment with people of "acceptable" character.

An important regulation helps prevent discrimination against people who may have been arrested for, but not convicted of, a crime. It prohibits inquiry as to whether a job applicant has ever been arrested. Questions concerning an applicant's *conviction* (and if so, when, where, and the disposition of the case) are allowed. No questions may be raised regarding your credit rating, charge accounts, or other financial matters. Finally, you may be asked about the type of education and experience you obtained in military service as it relates to a particular job, but you may not be asked what type of discharge you received. As you consider the various laws and rules that apply to the prevention of discrimination in hiring, remember that the law alone cannot create fairness and equity. Agencies such as the EEOC have been set up especially to enforce these regulations. The other essential element (besides the law and the agencies) needed to combat discrimination is *you*. You must be aware of your rights as well as the rights of others. If you feel discrimination is being practiced, you must take the steps to alert the involved parties.

SEXUAL HARASSMENT

Thus far, some highlights of your legal rights in employment have been discussed. This section is concerned with another type of discrimination—sexual harassment.

Sexual harassment in the workplace is conduct by another employee which focuses on an individual's sexual role at the expense of that individual's role as a worker. Sexual harassment may consist of looks or remarks, or it may go as far as physical assault. It can occur at any level of an organization. Supervisors may be harassed by subordinates as well as vice versa.

The consequences of such abuse can lead to a good deal of personal sacrifice. A person may feel obligated to quit a job due to harassment or may even be fired from the job for resistance. The equal opportunity laws and civil rights agencies provide help for those who feel they are being sexually harassed. If you feel you are being harassed on the job, remember that you have the *right* to be free from pressure or abuse. Some forms of harassment (such as physical assault) are crimes. Do not hesitate, in that case, to go to your local police department. If the form of harassment you encounter is not specifically a crime, there are other remedies. Unions and personnel departments can provide internal contacts. You may also file complaints on a federal level (with the EEOC) and on a local level (with human rights agencies). Finally, if you are being harassed, let the person know that this behavior is unacceptable. You have the right to resist!

DISCRIMINATING AMONG COWORKERS

Twenty years ago Elizabeth had been a very successful receptionist in a utility company. She had enjoyed her work and now was ready to return to the job market. She refreshed her professional skills by taking a computer class and a human relations class at a local community college. She prepared a resume, updated her references, and began the interviewing process. But things seemed different now. It seemed people were talking down to her—treating her with less respect. When she finally obtained a position, she found herself in the back office of the company doing data entry work where she had little contact with the public. After several weeks on the job, she explained to her boss that she would like to be moved to a position where she could meet the public. He mumbled something about, "We like to give the public an image of being a young, forward-looking company." Her coworkers didn't seem to enjoy the "goodies" she brought to break time. They made comments about the importance of being trim and fit. Elizabeth was aware that she had put on quite a few pounds over the past few years. What was Elizabeth's problem? Is there discrimination involved in this case?

The United States Constitution offers many kinds of protection from prejudice and discrimination. Many federal, state, and local regulations also contribute to the protection of our rights. But the attitudes, basic human nature, cannot be entirely controlled by legislation. Your attitudes and those of your coworkers will still be controlled by the mind and actions.

Subtle Discrimination

Discrimination not entirely covered by law may be just as harmful as the types of discrimination previously discussed in this chapter. This type of discrimination is often referred to as **subtle discrimination**. Subtle means not obvious and seldom brought out in the open. Subtle discrimination includes discrimination based on appearance, values, lifestyle, or some other personal factor.

In this category, we find discrimination against overweight people, short people, tall people, single people, divorced people, or recovering alcoholics, to name a few. You may be a victim of this type of discrimination, or you may be guilty of subtle discrimination against others. Subtle prejudices against others often occur as a result of tradition or habit. No harm is originally intended. Often you may not even be aware that you are discriminating against someone when this type of discrimination is involved.

A heavyset executive may not be promoted because that image is not the one the company wishes to project. The company may not have an "image" policy. But through tradition it has promoted—perhaps unknowingly—the

ILLUSTRATION 11-3.   A willingness to accept and try to understand others as they are helps you to avoid ruining a working relationship.

slim, athletic-looking male or female. As height is commonly associated with aggressiveness and self-confidence, a short person may not have a chance for promotion. The divorced woman may be passed over for promotion because the male executives in the office or their wives may feel uncomfortable with her in the executive suite. No one in the office goes to break with Phyllis. Phyllis is categorized as a "health food nut" and brings some unusual snacks.

If you find yourself a victim of this type of subtle discrimination, what should you do? If you wish to stay in the company, you need to find out if the discrimination factor holding you back can be changed. Arthur has noticed that the past five promotions have gone to very tall employees. Arthur is five feet, seven inches. There is little he can do about his height. If the difference is not something you can change, or something you choose not to change, you can only strive to excel in another area to make up the difference. Sometimes the change is easy and worth the effort. Teresa has observed that the operators in the word processing pool who have been moved to the executive offices have been well-dressed, polished-looking people. Teresa can change her image and increase her chances for promotion by updating her wardrobe and taking more time with her appearance.

If your future or happiness is blocked by subtle discrimination focusing on something you cannot change, you may want to consider looking for different employment or a new environment where you feel more accepted. Most importantly, do not let discrimination injure your self-esteem and thus limit your potential. You will find that your own prejudices disappear as you become more self-confident and less threatened by the progress of others.

AVOIDING, FIGHTING, OR RESISTING DISCRIMINATION

To this point we have considered the many different aspects of discrimination and prejudice in the work world. You have been encouraged to be alert and sensitive to discrimination and prejudice. Our concern now turns to dealing with actual discrimination. Keep in mind that prejudice and discrimination are destructive and can often be offset by developing tolerance and understanding for other individuals. Tolerant people are those who are secure and can separate the important from the unimportant. Does it really make a difference to you if Phyllis eats bean sprouts at break time? Should her eating habits really make a difference in how you feel about her? A willingness to accept and try to understand others as they are will go a long way in helping you preserve good working relationships.

There are several options available to you if you feel you are a victim of discrimination.

Turn and Walk Away

There may be situations where you consider the costs of confrontation too high when dealing with discrimination. You may feel that the least painful choice is to walk away from the pressure. You might resign your position or ask for a transfer to free yourself from a situation. You may even refuse a job offer, feeling that the pressure of prejudice from your subordinates or coworkers will be too great.

Simply turning and walking away *seems* like the least painful option, but it leaves you with little hope or satisfaction. In the long run, it can affect others who may be in your position. Prejudices will not be brought to light. Unfair practices will continue. And by leaving, you will be helping to maintain that prejudice. Keep your own rights in mind. Then, turning and walking away may not seem so painless.

Revenge

If you are a victim of discrimination, your first impulse may be to get even with the offender. This alternative usually does more harm than good.

Often it simply increases the prejudice and, as a result, the discrimination. Revenge can take many forms—from vandalizing to physical assault. Be aware of the consequences. They are far more damaging than any pleasure you may receive from getting even. Recognize the folly of revenge.

Positive Resistance with Patience

Occasionally you can overcome prejudice with time and patience. The very nature of *prejudice*—based on stereotypes of the individual or the group—is not only unfair. Most often it is not even an accurate picture. Demonstrating that you do not fit the image, by doing your best job, can do much to reduce or eliminate the prejudice. For instance, when Elizabeth reorganized the entire filing system, eliminating the problem of misindexed files, her coworkers began to seek her advice. They no longer emphasized the difference in age. They no longer avoided contact with her.

Positive resistance does not mean that you should ignore or endure the prejudice. **Positive resistance** means clearly recognizing *and* confronting the prejudice. It means letting your coworkers know that you are aware of the prejudice and are uncomfortable with it—but determined to prove them wrong. Unfortunately, not all discrimination can be eliminated with positive resistance. The last section deals with the strongest means of dealing with discrimination.

Come Right Out and Fight

This chapter has discussed your basic human rights. These rights are protected by laws and regulations of our government. If you feel your rights are being violated, you have remedies under the law for dealing with this discrimination.

Your first action should be to attempt to correct the situation from an on-the-job perspective. Contact a member of your personnel department or union. An investigation will be conducted. If just cause is found, grievance procedures can be initiated. This may be as far as you need to go to correct the discrimination. If you receive no satisfaction from these sources, your next step will be to contact either an attorney or a governmental agency dealing with discrimination. On a local level, you may contact any human rights agency. On the federal level, you should contact the Equal Employment Opportunity Commission (EEOC). Be aware that if you have a legal case against your employer for discrimination, you must be prepared to face a not-always-sympathetic public, often including your coworkers. If you decide to proceed with court remedies, don't make it a halfhearted attempt. Backing away after you have taken the initiative can be worse than losing. Always keep in mind your right to be judged for yourself—free of stereotypes and prejudices. You have the right to fight discrimination.

QUESTIONS AND PROJECTS

1. Finish the following sentences with your first thoughts. Share your answers with a classmate. As you review the answers, examine them for prejudicial thoughts.

    a. Tourists are _____.

    b. Bosses are _____.

    c. Alcoholics are _____.

    d. Cab drivers are _____.

    e. Farmers are _____.

    f. Old people are _____.

    g. Red heads are _____.

    h. Hairdressers are _____.

    i. Cats are _____.

    j. Welfare recipients are _____.

2. Can you think of any instances in which you were prejudiced against someone because the person didn't fit the "right image" in your peer group? Describe one of those situations to someone.

3. Search out a documented case of discrimination in the workplace. Newspapers, magazines, or records of court cases may be helpful to you. Study the case and write a report on it. Present the case in class.

4. Write up a list of questions which you feel would be discriminatory in an employment interview. Check with a legal authority to find out which of your questions would be illegal.

5. Discuss in a small group how you would respond to an employer who asked you questions during the employment interview which you know are discriminatory and illegal.

6. Interview or invite as a guest speaker a personnel director of a public agency to explain the agency's affirmative action plan. Perhaps the personnel director will be willing to share a copy of the plan. Be prepared to ask specific questions about the plan and its impact on the workplace.

For example: Who wrote the plan? Who sees the plan? What changes have been made in the agency since the plan was adopted?

7. Write a paper or prepare a speech on the topic, "How can tolerance and understanding help overcome the negative effects of prejudice and discrimination?"

CASE PROBLEMS

1. Sex Discrimination.

Reread the story of Judy, Tom, and Mr. Aubrey at the beginning of this chapter.

    a. Put yourself in Judy's position. What action could you have taken to have prevented or corrected this situation?

    b. Put yourself in Tom's position. What are your responsibilities as a coworker to Judy? What are your responsibilities to Mr. Aubrey? What steps might you take to help correct the situation?

2. Age Discrimination.

After receiving an outstanding application for the position of teller at Security First Bank, the personnel director decided to call Charles Nelson in for an interview. Charles walked into the managerial offices of the bank the morning of the interview. The personnel director entered the outer office and saw Charles. He said, "Sir, these are the managerial offices. The tellers are located in the front section of the bank." Charles replied, "I'm here for an interview with the personnel director." The director looked at the floor for a minute and then said, "Quite truthfully, I had no idea . . . Your age . . . " What could Charles Nelson do?

3. Modeling?

Alice had graduated from a two-year fashion merchandising program and obtained a good position as an executive trainee for a large department store. Her main job was salesperson in the camera department. The store advertising manager, George Smith, asked Alice to model in some of the store's newspaper ads. During one of the picture-taking sessions, George Smith appeared and stayed for the entire session. After the session, he walked over to Alice and said, "I'm working on a swimsuit promotion and doing the photography myself. It's not really for the store. How would you like to pick up a few extra dollars by working overtime on this project?" There was a pause.

    a. Are there any clues in this case to indicate something about George Smith's motives?

b. What are the important questions that Alice must answer as she considers how to respond to George Smith?

4. Someone New.

Merna Masters has been working as a designer at a top fashion house in New York for several years. Her record as an employee is excellent, but she has a tendency to worry about her job. As she had dinner with a friend, Merna said, "I think I'm in for real trouble." "What's the problem?" her friend asked. Merna replied, "They have added another designer in my division—a young French woman. The boss probably wanted someone who will work twenty-four hours a day and all weekend. You know how those foreigners are. She'll probably work for next to nothing." Her friend responded, "I don't know why you are so concerned. You are very talented and constantly complimented on your work." Merna said, "And her accent is ridiculous. You'd think that if she were going to live here she could learn to speak the language. I don't know why they couldn't have hired one of the hundreds of local designers who are dying to get into the business."

a. What seems to be Merna's problem with the new designer?
b. How would you recommend that Merna go about changing her attitude?
c. If you were Merna's friend, what advice would you give her?

12

Establishing Communication Channels

LEARNING OBJECTIVES:

1. Understand the definition and importance of good communication.
2. Know the barriers to good communication.
3. Understand some techniques to opening communication channels.
4. Know the importance of assertive behavior and its impact on communication.
5. Develop the techniques of good listening.

"Hello, Howard. What's new in your department this morning?"

"Oh, nothing much. We are expecting a big shipment of supplies around ten this morning. That should keep us busy for several hours."

"Jake, did you hear about Adelaine? She slipped on the stairs to the Shipping Department yesterday. I heard that the steps were in need of repair. She fell all the way to the bottom. Rumor has it that she has a concussion and broken leg."

"Yeah, Howard, I heard that scoop. Sounds like she's going to sue the company for big bucks."

"Who did you hear that from?"
*"Some guy who works in Shipping. He said he heard it
from Adelaine's neighbor."*

___*Communication* in the workplace comes from a wide
variety of sources and takes place in a variety of settings. Communication in
written form may come from letters, memos, company periodicals, or bulletin
board messages. Oral communication comes from supervisors, coworkers,
suppliers, customers, and perhaps even the competition. The rumor, or "the
grapevine," provides you with the daily gossip. Yes, rumors are a source of
communication. This type of communication is illustrated concerning
Adelaine. (The truth of this story is that Adelaine slipped in the shipping
room. She was taken to the hospital and found to have no physical problems resulting from the fall.) The body motions of others also provide us
with information. Even the body shape and clothing of others communicates
a message to us. With all these forms of communication available to us, it is,
at first glance, amazing that communication continues to be a problem in
the workplace as well as in our daily lives.

WHAT IS COMMUNICATION?

There are two key individuals involved in the communication process.
The **sender** of information is the one with the thought or idea which is to
be transmitted to another. The **receiver** is the individual who is to receive
the thought, which is referred to as the **message**. Communication takes
place when the message transferred from the sender to the receiver is *shared*

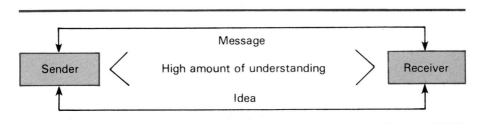

FIGURE 12-1.   Communication

and *understood*. Sharing indicates that communication involves more than one person. There must be one who sends the information and one who reacts to it. Understanding means that both the sender and the receiver share the same meaning of what is being said.

Communication is often said to be the foremost problem in the workplace. This statement is likely very accurate because often senders and receivers do not share the same understanding of the message and communication does not take place. There are many barriers to the communication process. Barriers do not allow a message to be shared.

OVERCOMING BARRIERS TO COMMUNICATION

The first step in overcoming barriers to communication is to recognize them. The most common barrier is a poor choice of words. Words have varied meanings. What a word means to one person may mean an entirely different thing to another person. Take the word "tough," for example. One person may use it to describe somebody they consider rough, mean, and strong. Another person may use the term to compliment someone highly who is great looking or who has other desirable traits.

ILLUSTRATION 12–1. When you are in doubt about how someone is interpreting your thoughts, ask! Thus, a step is made toward eliminating a barrier to communication.

You should strive to use words that will not be misunderstood. Select words that you feel have the same meaning and feeling to the other person. With some words, that can be very difficult. A word like "sleazy," for example, has the same feeling tone to most of us. But other words, such as "establishment" and "liberal," may have a negative or positive tone, depending on a person's background and experience. If you are in doubt about how someone is interpreting your thoughts, ask! This is a step toward eliminating a barrier to communication.

It would be simple if all emotionally charged words were reacted to by everyone in the same way. You could then deliberately avoid using dangerous words. Of course, such a simple solution is not possible. You say what you say because you are the kind of person you are. In other words, you speak through something referred to as a **filter**. Furthermore, you hear what other people say through that same filter. Someone else, with a different makeup and different experiences—and thus a different filter—will pick out different meanings from those same words. If you are suspicious by nature, you think other people are suspicious, too. You read into any statement made to you some part of your own characteristics.

Selective Communication

Many of us are guilty of selective communication. We hear what we want to hear and read what we want to read. Most of us like to skip the unpleasant things in life, particularly if they are a threat to the way we like to think of ourselves, our beliefs and convictions, and thoughts. Each of us has had the experience of trying to persuade friends to abandon foolish ideas in favor of our sensible ones. The friends resort to a simple and effective countermeasure; they do not hear our arguments. We all have equal access to these selective communication devices.

Acceptance

The hardest lesson to be learned as you attempt to open communication channels with other people is that change can come only through the wishes of the person involved. You may see others acting foolishly, making mistakes, or taking the wrong turn. You may have made some of the same mistakes yourself, and your natural tendency is to point out the error of their ways. You will learn, however, that you cannot change others through pointing out their faults. In fact, such a step usually makes matters worse. Change comes because the person wants to change—and through no other way. The principle involved in changing someone is *acceptance*—acceptance of yourself and acceptance of others.

Accept Yourself. What does "accept yourself" mean? Simply this: Work every day—for just a few minutes at a time—to accept yourself the way you are. Don't dwell on your faults; just accept them. Say to yourself, "Yes, I know you put things off until the last minute. I know you are sarcastic whenever you are afraid someone is going to hurt you. I know you are afraid to take the first step in getting acquainted with another person. But I like you anyway." Do you know what happens when you accept yourself the way you are? With acceptance comes the ability to change. As long as you defend yourself, make excuses, or blame your troubles on others, you will be unable to change. You will have a mental paralysis that literally keeps you from getting rid of any of the qualities within you that are hurting your chances for success and happiness.

When you take that one hard step of acceptance, however, you seem to release a brake inside of you. No longer will you be driving yourself with your brakes on. You will be free from the drag of that nonacceptance brake. With that brake released, you will find it easier to change. Don't forget, though, that accepting yourself is not easy. It is, in fact, terribly hard. Don't try to build self-acceptance too quickly. Just work at it for a few minutes at a time. One psychologist has mentioned five minutes as the goal you should set. For five minutes at a time, look at yourself squarely. Say, "Yes, that's the way I am. But I'm still OK."

Accept Others. The second step in acceptance seems to follow the first one naturally. After you have learned to accept yourself, you can begin to accept others. When you have learned to look squarely at your own faults, without criticism, you can look at the shortcomings of others without trying to change them. The "brake release" effect seems to work with others just as well as it does with you. When you can look at your bullying customer and say, "This customer is angry with me, but it may be caused by something else. This customer is a good person underneath," you will release your customer's brake. Laura Huxley has written a book called *You Are Not the Target*.[1] This book says that most of the cruel things said to others are not really directed at them. The person "picked on" may have just been around

---

1. Laura Huxley, *You are Not the Target: Transforming Negative Feelings into Creative Action Harmonious Relationships* (Los Angeles: Jeremy P. Tarcher, Inc., 1986).

when the speaker defended himself or herself by lashing out at the closest person. When *you do not defend yourself*, but merely accept others for what they are, your attitude will tell others that you are still their friend. When they feel your accepting attitude, in spite of what they have said or done, they will be able to release the brake that is holding them back. They will be able to change.

Improve Your Awareness

Awareness is especially important when you work in groups. Awareness means that you are conscious of the feelings and personalities of the people who work with you. You know which areas can be discussed with your coworkers and which should be left alone. You know when others would rather not talk and when they would welcome an invitation to lunch. If you are aware of others, you will spend more of your time looking outside yourself instead of looking inward. Awareness grows as you become less self-centered.

Awareness has another side, as well. Be aware of the flow of authority in the firm in which you work. This means that you will go through **channels.** You will take your questions and problems to your immediate supervisor. That person carries them to the next level of management, and so on. If you should go over the head of your immediate supervisor, you fail to show respect for this position. You should study the organization chart of the firm. It lists the officers of the company, the heads of departments, supervisors, and so on. You will then know how the whole organization works; you will also have a clearer picture of your position. This will show you the communication paths downward and upward for directions, information, suggestions, and grievances. It will also show you where your work ultimately goes, a knowledge that adds to your feeling of worth.

Empathy

It isn't what you say, it's the way you say it that sometimes makes the difference. If you are to improve **tone,** or the way you say it, you must work to develop the trait of **empathy.** To have empathy means to see and feel something just the way another person sees and feels it. In a sense, you feel with the other person. For example, if you are walking down the street with a friend and that friend has a hole in his or her shoe and you can feel the breeze, you have empathy. You may think that there is no room in the workplace for empathy, but this is not true. What you will probably find is too little time for an expression of empathy. In any case, you should be concerned with being empathetic yourself, not with having others empathize with you.

You will have many opportunities to show understanding and empathy. If you are sensitive to the feelings of others, you will try to make them feel at ease. The ability to make others feel at ease is an important factor in getting along with others. It also helps them to feel at ease about sharing their real inner feelings with you. If you are relaxed and natural yourself, it is because you are able to think of others instead of yourself.

In addition to putting others at ease, be careful to treat others as you would like to be treated. Speak in a friendly manner to new employees; take the time to be kind to those who are in trouble; be sensitive to moods and do not intrude on another's privacy.

The Art of Persuasion

The art of persuasion is basically the art of breaking down barriers to communication—gently or forcibly—so that your message can get through. You have been using techniques of persuasion in your work and play all

ILLUSTRATION 12–2.   When your work brings you into contact with many people, a friendly attitude is essential to good communication.

through your life. You have learned that some techniques are effective and some are not. At the age of three or four, you may have tried the technique of lying on the floor and screaming to get your own way. You may have discovered, too, that this didn't work too well at age nine or ten. In this same way, you may have tried and discarded many techniques of persuasion. You should sharpen up some techniques you now use and perhaps become familiar with some entirely new ones.

CHANNEL OPENERS

It is very important to establish a rapport with others which will be conducive to the communication process. This can be done with a friendly smile, a positive attitude, and an attempt to understand others. If people are comfortable with you and feel that you care, they will be more likely to open up and communicate with you. The sharing and understanding which are so vital to good communication will more likely occur if you have established a positive set.

> *One slow stormy afternoon, a comfortably dressed man came on to Wally's car lot. One of the older salespeople said, "I don't think he has any money anyway." But one of the newer salespeople stepped forward with a friendly hello and showed the man several of the newer models available. Then, as the experienced salesperson predicted, the man left without buying a car. A few days later, however, the new salesperson was surprised and pleased when the man came in and specifically asked to see him. The man purchased for cash two late model vehicles for his children.*

A Friendly Attitude

A friendly personality is an asset to communication. If your work brings you into contact with many people, a friendly attitude is essential. If you are gifted with a liking for people, you should do well. But if strangers make you want to "back off," don't give up. The technique of being courteous is a good way to begin working on creating a friendly and more outgoing personality. At first, you will have to work at it. Take every opportunity to say "thank you" with a smile. Look for the good in others. You will find that each new acquaintance will bring a new dimension to your life.

Study Others

Why do people behave as they do? In other words, why do people act like people? Most people who have watched television shows and have read popular articles can tell you all about inferiority complexes, depression, overcompensation, and so on. Most psychologists, however, realize that there is still much to learn about the nature of people. They dislike giving the impression that human nature is an open book. Still, research continues at an ever-increasing rate, and more and more complexities of people are being understood. We do know some of the factors causing behavior. Some of them are conditioning, or building up habitual responses to certain words, rules, and other stimuli. Some examples of these are illnesses (particularly those affecting the nervous system), conflicts (both conscious and unconscious), and the pressures exerted by the different groups that are active in a person's life.

Such knowledge of psychology is helpful in understanding ourselves and others. This type of information is needed as we try to improve our lines of communication with others.

Use the Positive Approach

If you want to persuade someone to do something, you will be more successful if the discussion is positive or pleasant. If others like you as a person, they will be more willing to listen to what you have to say. The best way to keep your dealings with others as pleasant as you can is to look for "yes" situations and to watch out for the things that have unpleasant consequences.

Help the Other Person Feel Important

You will not succeed if you build yourself up at the expense of other people. If you boast about how well you are doing, you will make others feel doubtful about their own success. If you treat others as if you were on a higher plane, you will again make them doubt their own value. For example, if you begin by saying, "You may not understand this, but . . . ," you will make your listener feel smaller. Another statement that causes your listener to feel small is to say, "It ought to be perfectly clear that . . . " The way to make others feel tall and important is to ask for their advice, to get their point of view, to make them a part of any decision you make. Look for opportunities to give recognition, to build others up, to make them feel ten feet tall.

An important technique in helping others to feel important is learning how to play second fiddle. This may seem odd, yet it is effective. If you watch successful salespeople, for example, you will notice their easy, relaxed manner. This manner sets the stage; it provides the kind of atmosphere needed in selling. If this atmosphere is friendly, if the customer feels important, and if the salesperson can explain the product and answer questions intelligently and courteously, the customer will feel free to choose but will be much more likely to choose—in favor of the salesperson.

Ignore the Negative

When others complain about your actions or job performance, let them talk. Just listen attentively. As you listen, ignore the part of the conversation that sounds as if it is directed at you personally. Negative statements of this kind are best forgotten. Just concentrate on what you can learn and give the complainer the opportunity to speak.

Reward the Positive

When someone says something positive about you or your company, respond warmly. Such a response is rewarding to the other person, and you have learned from previous chapters that rewarded responses are more likely to be repeated than those that are not rewarded. Most of us have trouble, however, in accepting compliments. Practice saying something warm, something "giving" back to the person who compliments you. Instead of saying, "Oh, it was nothing," show the other person how the compliment made you feel. If you say, "It makes me feel good to hear you say that," you are giving the other person warmth in return for those kind words to you. Accepting compliments warmly takes practice, and it is never too late to begin.

Be Mindful of Gossip

In your effort to keep channels of communication open, keep in mind that a very powerful channel of information in any organization is gossip (referred to as the rumor mill or the grapevine). Gossip is found in all workplaces. The important thing to remember is that gossip starts where information stops. It seems that gossip springs up when people are curious about a situation and they cannot get the facts. When this happens, speculation begins and the grapevine goes into full force. As a worker, it is important for you to listen to gossip which may be well founded about policies affecting the workplace. It is best not to repeat the gossip but rather to ask someone to give you the straight information. Malicious gossip about individuals should be ignored or shared with others who can put a stop to it.

ASSERTIVE COMMUNICATION

A special skill referred to as **assertiveness** is often needed in the workplace. Assertiveness is the ability to communicate your rights to others without stepping on the rights of others. A person who is assertive has the skill of stating ideas and feelings openly in an interpersonally effective manner. Let's review a little more closely what is meant by assertive through example.

If you order a rare steak in a fine restaurant, you have every right to expect that a rare steak will be placed before you. If the steak is delivered to you cooked well done, and you accept the steak without comment, you have displayed **passive** behavior. Passive behavior indicates that you give in to the demands of others, even when doing so is inconvenient or against your best interests. If you act passively, you serve as a "doormat" for others, never standing up for your rights. The danger in acting passively is that you will fail to describe or to express anger and other feelings; the outcome may be resentment, depression, or illness.

The opposite of passive behavior is **aggressive** behavior. If the steak is delivered to you cooked well done, and you shout that this steak is not acceptable and pound the table, you embarrass yourself, your dining partner, people at other tables, and the waitress. You have communicated your feelings in an aggressive manner. Aggressive behavior is highly defensive. It is fault-finding and judgmental. This type of reaction certainly communicates your feelings, but you step on the rights of others in the process.

Assertive behavior would dictate that you would point out to the waitress that you had ordered a rare steak. You would ask that the steak be returned to the kitchen and replaced. Assertive behavior is somewhere between passive and aggressive behavior. Being assertive allows you to share your ideas and feelings in a positive way. Many people avoid being assertive because they think they are not important or they feel guilty about their

ILLUSTRATION 12-3.
Assertiveness is the
ability to communicate
your rights to others
without stepping on the
rights of others.

emotions. Everyone is important. It doesn't matter if you are a shop super-visor, a president of a bank, a student, a housekeeper, or a sanitation engineer—you are important. Any feeling you have is your feeling and you should not feel guilty about having it. To use assertive language you should identify what you are thinking or feeling and state it in the most interper-sonally sound way possible.

The way you conduct yourself while being assertive is also important if you are to state effectively what you believe to be true for you. You take the responsibility for your actions and feelings, and you do not attack another individual personally. In addition to stating your feelings and saying the right words, you will need to:

1. Establish good eye contact with the person you are communicating with. Eye contact is important. It is an indication to others that you mean what you say. If you have a difficult time looking peo-ple in the eye, start working on this skill. (You may want to start out by talking to noses, and then work you way up to the eyes.)

2. Body position is also important. If you are going to be assertive, position yourself so that, as nearly as possible, your eyes will be on the same level as the person to whom you are communicating assertively. If the recipient of your message is sitting, you sit. If he or she is standing, you stand. Be careful not to get too far into the "space" of the other person, as this may be interpreted as aggressive behavior.

3. Avoid the use of gestures which may be interpreted as aggressive. No finger pointing or quick moves.

4. Your voice tone should be normal. Be sure that you speak clearly and loudly enough for the person you are communicating with to hear you.

The art of being assertive takes thought and practice. It is important to get the words and the body language working together to convey a message. Remember that passive people are often unhappy as a result of not stating what they think and feel; aggressive people get their ideas and feelings heard but may create more problems for themselves because of their behavior.

LISTENING TO COMMUNICATE

In your daily communication, more time is spent in listening than in reading, speaking, or writing. Yet little emphasis is generally placed on the skill of listening in the education process. Listening is an art that should be practiced every day. Research studies have shown that many of us hear, but we do not listen. *Listening is the process by which we make sense out of what we hear.* If you want to improve the communication skill of listening, you should:

1. Prepare yourself to listen.
2. Learn to shift from speaker to listener.
3. Listen actively and take well-organized notes.
4. Avoid emotional responses.
5. Avoid the common stumbling blocks of good listening.

Prepare Yourself to Listen

The efficiency of your listening will improve if you prepare yourself both mentally and physically to listen. Stop thinking about the hundreds of miscellaneous thoughts which may be running through your mind. If the supervisor is explaining a new procedure, erase competing thoughts from your mind—what was said at break, the car repair bill you have to pay, and your plans for the weekend. You cannot act on any of those thoughts now. Just forget them and prepare to listen. Stand or sit in a way that will help you listen. Being physically alert will help the process. Look the speaker in the eye as you prepare yourself. A visual bond between the sender of a message and the receiver is important in listening.

Shift from Speaker to Listener

In conversation communication, the switch of roles from speaker to listener and back to speaker are frequent. In the switching of roles, it is important that you spend your time listening and not preparing your next speech. If, as you are supposed to be listening, you are thinking of something clever to say or trying to determine what questions you will ask when the speaker is finished, the message of the speaker will be lost. The next time you are involved in a conversation, check yourself—are you preparing a speech or listening?

Listen Actively and Take Well-Organized Notes

One of the reasons many people are not good listeners is because the listener thinks faster than most people talk. Therefore, listeners have extra time which enables the mind to wander back to thinking about other things. Use this time as "think" time. You should use these moments to paraphrase and interpret mentally what is being said. This active type of listening requires hard work, but the rewards will be great.

Another part of being an active listener is to take notes. Notetaking is not always appropriate or possible, but whenever you can jot down some notes for later reference, do so. Avoid trying to take down too much. Listen a lot and write a little. Put down only the main points of what the speaker is saying. If you spend too much time getting everything down, you will be sure to miss some of the main points. Review your notes as soon as possible. At that time you may want to add to them and put them in good order.

As an active listener, you will want to encourage the speaker, in some settings, with a follow-up. This will help you keep alert and allow you to probe for additional information. It may be important to clarify what has been said. This is done in an effort to get a definition or further explanation about a word, thought, or phrase. Speaker says, "I'll tell you that my cognitive powers are slow today." Listener attempts to understand and clarify: "What do you mean by cognitive powers?" A deliberate attempt on the part of the listener to pull together the main points of the speaker is also a good technique. The listener might reply, "Let me see if I have it straight,

ILLUSTRATION 12-4.   Good eye contact helps the active listener to concentrate and make sense out of what is heard.

first." An echo response is also a good technique for an active listener. You simply repeat what has been said by the speaker. This reinforces the information for you and indicates to the speaker that you have been listening.

Avoid Emotional Responses

Many times as you listen it is difficult to control your emotional responses to the speaker's message. Each of us has a list of words that trigger an emotional response. What are some words that cause an emotional reaction for you? Perhaps some of these words on your list include "libber," "Democrat," "Republican," "Communist," or "weirdo." Poor listeners spend their time reacting to "red flag" words. When this happens, the message is lost. If you want to improve your listening skills, you will work hard to remain objective.

Avoid the Stumbling Blocks

There are some common stumbling blocks which interfere with the listening process. *Daydreaming* falls in this category. This habit can become an enemy to your effort to develop good listening skills. When you feel your attention wandering, snap it back to where it should be focused. This takes a conscious effort. Begin to jot notes down on what is presently being said, and don't worry about what you missed while daydreaming. Perhaps you can figure it out later. *Attending to distractions* is another stumbling block. Street noises, latecomers, whispering, or a child in the audience may shift your thoughts away from the main message. Sometimes the speaker is a distraction—an unusual appearance, the pronunciation of a word, or a unique voice may catch your attention and shatter the listening process. *Criticizing the delivery of the message* can fall in this group of bad habits. It is possible to get so caught up in criticizing the presenter's delivery that you fail to absorb the content. To all of these distractions, you must turn a deaf ear. Concentrate on the content of the message. Let all unimportant matters go. Remember, too, that listening is work. Be sure to work at it when you listen.

QUESTIONS AND PROJECTS

1. One of the most difficult ways of becoming more outgoing is taking the initiative in meeting new people. To help you overcome this universal tendency toward ''inwardness,'' you are to meet entirely through your own effects, ten people (of any age). Exactly four weeks from today you are to report the results of the project on a separate sheet of paper in the following form:

Name	Short Biography	Situation (How We Met)	Opener (What I Said)
1.			
2.			
3.			

Remember, you must have ten names and *you* must make the first move. No one else may introduce you. The short biography should contain at least four items of information about each person.

Follow your report with a paragraph of evaluation of the experience. How did it affect you? Will it change your future behavior? What have you learned about people in general?

2. Start this message around to a group of five or six people. (Play gossip or telephone as you did as a child.) "The President of the company will be in the Personnel Department on Tuesday, August 14, at 2:30 p.m. with department heads. He will meet with any personnel desiring to discuss problems on Wednesday, August 15, at 9:00 a.m. If you wish to speak to the President, inform your supervisor." After the last person has received the information, compare inal message. Discuss why and how information was distorted.

3. Emily arrives late to a large lecture session on vacations in Italy. Because all the seats in the front area are occupied, she takes a seat in the back of the room. She notices two people in front of her talking noisily. She assumes they will quiet down when the lecturer arrives and begins the program. Several minutes into the session, however, they are still talking. Emily is missing some important points because of the noise level. Role-play with others how Emily might react to this situation in an aggressive manner. Then try it again with Emily responding in an assertive manner.

4. You have a friend who is extremely interested in current politics. In order to carry on an intelligent conversation, go over one of the news magazines for this week. Choose five topics that might interest your friend and learn something about each topic.

5. The next time you are talking with a friend, try this experiment: See if you can remain silent exactly half the time. You may need to spur your friend with such remarks as, "And then what happened?" See if you are talking too much or too little as a general rule.

6. Which of the following descriptions would you use to describe the way you meet people during an interview? What can you do to improve your rating?

_____ Lacks ease	_____ Slightly nervous	_____ Averted eye
_____ Nervous	_____ At ease	_____ Great poise

7. Make a list of ten words you use occasionally that have an unpleasant emotional connotation or coloring. Next, see if you can find a synonym for each of the ten words, each synonym to have a pleasant connotation. Try to make the pleasant words a part of your vocabulary, at the same time eliminating the unpleasant words.

8. Practice the suggestions given in the "Listening to Communicate" section in this chapter in one of your lecture classes. Do you think that this method of taking notes has helped you? Discuss.

9. Begin a conversation with someone whose remarks usually irritate you. Let the other person talk; you listen. Do not interrupt for at least three minutes. See if you can detect *why* this person holds these beliefs, if there is some logical basis for this point of view. Now, answer with a compromising statement, such as, ''You do have a point there, but what do you think about . . . ?'' Ask an intelligent question, one that shows you were really listening. Did this activity improve your relationship with this particular person? Discuss.

CASE PROBLEMS

1. Word Lack or Judgment Lack?

Alex Curtis took dictation from Joan Grayson, the head of the advertising department. Joan was a rapid speaker and occasionally slurred words to the point that Alex could not understand them. One day during dictation, Joan used the word *hybrid*, but Alex heard the word as *high-bred*. Not getting the idea, Alex interrupted, ''Ms. Grayson, do you mean high-bred?'' Joan was annoyed at losing her train of thought. ''Use better judgment,'' she said, ''and don't interrupt.''

a. Assuming that Alex had been working at this position for more than six months, is there some way he could have avoided this situation?
b. How should Alex have reacted to this reprimand?
c. What clues should he have had from the context to help him in deciding which word was intended?

2. The Seamy Side.

Louise Ryan is a secretary for a small-town newspaper publisher. One part of her job is to keep subscribers and advertisers satisfied as far as possible and to try to create a feeling of goodwill between publisher and the community. One day, when she answers the telephone, a voice demands to talk to the managing editor. Louise replies that the managing editor is not in the office and asks if she can help. The person answers in a loud voice, using abusive language. Louise puts the receiver down with a bang. The telephone rings for some time, but she refuses to listen again to such talk.

a. What is the correct attitude toward difficult individuals in situations such as this one?
b. Was Louise behaving in an objective manner?
c. Why do you think Louise acted as she did?
d. What might have Louise done that would have served the publisher in a better way?

3. A Place for Sensitivity.

Ann Madison is responsible for admitting patients in a large medical clinic. Her task is to fill out routine records concerning patients for the files. The data are of a factual nature and contain no medical information. When talking with a middle-aged man, she observes that he is embarrassed by having to supply such information as his name, age, address, and business. When she has recorded these answers, Ann says to the patient, "And now will you tell me why you have come here?"

"Look, lady," he answers, "is it the practice for a patient to have to give you that kind of information?"

Ann answers, "I'm sorry, sir. I'm only doing my job. My instructions from Dr. Reynolds are that I must get this information."

    a.   Do you feel that Ann was sensitive to the needs of others?

    b.   About what types of needs or feelings are some people very sensitive?

    c.   Should Ann have insisted that the man answer her question? How would you have handled this situation? Why?

13

Getting Your Message Across

LEARNING OBJECTIVES:

1. Understand the importance of the ability to carry on a conversation.

2. Develop the ability to get feedback from listeners.

3. Know the requirements of carrying on a conversation.

4. Establish the ability to open a conversation.

5. Develop an awareness of the aids to good communication skills.

6. Develop an awareness of the importance of being able to speak before groups.

Ward and June were enjoying their coffee break when George walked in and said "hi" as he poured a cup of coffee and left. "What's with him? He doesn't ever say much more than 'hi' and 'goodbye,' " said June. Ward answered, "Either he is a snob, shy, or just a non-communicative person—I'm not sure which." June said, "I think he wants to be communicative with others. I have noticed that he watches others, looks longingly at the groups gathering at the water cooler, and smiles pleasantly at coworkers. I have attempted to talk to him, but the conversation always seems to drop in my lap. He just seems to avoid conversation settings." Ward responded,

> *"Well, maybe we can help him."* What could Ward and June do to help George?

___*What* is your greatest social fear? Wearing the wrong clothes? Probably not. Most people are much less concerned over fashion than they were in the past. Table etiquette? No. The casual mode of entertaining has almost eliminated worry about which fork to use. The one fear nearly everyone has is that of carrying on a conversation with someone who is not a close friend or member of the family. The difficulty arises when we must talk with those we know slightly, or perhaps not at all. You may be fearful, ill at ease, afraid you will be judged by what you say.

OVERCOMING FEAR OF CONVERSATION

How can we overcome fear of conversation? Actually, the secret of success in oral communication is one that has been mentioned before—just being yourself. Part of the strain that causes feelings of uneasiness stems from trying to impress others with a false personality. But if we pretend to be what we are not, we must be constantly on guard. This guardedness may be thought by others to be an attack against some weakness of their own. They, then, will defend themselves with similar pretenses. This vicious circle can produce nothing but disaster.

Don't Just Stand There—Say Something!

You have already learned that the human element is the most important one in business. If you can get along successfully with others, you will have many of the qualities you need for success. Most of getting along with others involves conversation. You must ask others to do things for you; you must express appreciation for a kindness; you must persuade a sales prospect; you must put your customer or caller at ease. All of this involves conversation. The importance of your ability to establish friendly relations with others cannot be overemphasized. Much of your success and happiness will depend on it. Some of the specific areas in your business life where conversational skill will help you are discussed in this chapter.

Improving Personal Relations

You will improve your relations with others if you improve your conversational skills. The secret lies in making your listener feel important. If you just talk about yourself and your own accomplishments, you probably will be considered a bore. If you talk sincerely about the accomplishments of your listener, you will have a fascinated audience. All people are interested in themselves; few feel properly appreciated. There is a story about a woman, Juanita, who picked ten names at random from the telephone directory and sent them telegrams with a one-word message, "Congratulations." She signed her name and address to the wire and awaited results. Nine of the ten individuals wrote her warm letters of thanks. All of them stated they had not been aware that anyone knew of their recent accomplishments. Only one person wrote to ask, "Congratulations for what?"

GETTING AND GIVING INFORMATION

Another way conversational skill can aid you is in giving and getting information. The business owner, the teacher, the supervisor—all must have the ability to talk conversationally to those whom they wish to instruct. Getting feedback is involved here, too; it is a two-way process. If you can ask sensible questions, if you can show with a nod or a smile that you understand, you will be using your conversational talents to advantage.

Try the following to encourage feedback from your listener so that two-way conversation takes place:

1. Give reinforcement to the listener who responds to your request for feedback. For example, suppose you ask a coworker how he or she likes the way you have rearranged the office and get the response: "The office looks cluttered this way," If you say, "Well, arrange it yourself," your coworker will probably terminate the conversation, and future two-way conversation will be minimal. To encourage future feedback you might have said, "Thanks for your help—how can I diminish the cluttered look?" In this way you encourage and strengthen two-way dialogue.

2. Outline the kind of feedback you are seeking. Avoid asking very general or vague questions about ideas, feelings, or behaviors; phrase your questions specifically. Instead of saying to a coworker, "Let me know if there is any way I can help you," try being specific. "Do you want help with the cash disbursement ledger or the mailing of statements?"

3. Avoid contradictions between your verbal and nonverbal cues. For instance, if you ask your carpool rider, "How are you this morning?" but your voice tone and expression indicate that you do not

really want to know, the other person may be reluctant to continue on with the conversation and the "give and take" process will stop.

Conversation is an aid to getting work done. If you can write conversationally, large groups will give you closer attention. If you can talk to your staff conversationally, they will be more likely to follow your directions. A good conversationalist creates a climate in which others feel comfortable in giving feedback.

ELEVEN EASY LESSONS IN CONVERSATION

It is all very well to say you should be able to converse with others with ease. But such a statement is certain to bring the question "How?" The following paragraphs will tell you how; after that, you just need practice.

You Must Like People

If you don't like people in general, this will be your first task. It is helpful if you realize that *everyone* is insecure to some degree. So if you feel insecure about liking others, you are not the only one who feels as you do. One of the best ways of starting your campaign to like people is to act as if you already did. You will be surprised at the reaction of others. You may even begin to like them!

Don't Talk Too Fast

Good conversation should be relaxing, so don't talk too fast. Otherwise your feelings of tenseness will be transmitted to your listeners. A good way to slow your speaking tempo down is by frequent pauses. Don't be afraid of silence. Constant chatter can be extremely wearing, and an occasional pause will point up what is said afterward. Clear enunciation is important. If you speak with a relaxed manner and with clear enunciation, you will find others listening to you. Your words will take on a new importance from your method of delivery.

Learn to Listen

One of the hardest lessons to learn is that of listening, but it is one of the most important. Specific suggestions about how to do this are found in the previous chapter. If you will think of your conversational group as a basketball team, for example, it may help you see the necessity of giving

ILLUSTRATION 13-1.   Good conversation is relaxing. When you talk too fast, your tense feelings are transmitted to your listeners.

each player a chance at the basket. Throw the conversational ball to others; listen with concentration; show your interest in your face. Learning this one lesson well can make others think you are a gifted conversationalist. You won't need to say much yourself if you can make the conversation of others seem more important. A good listener must keep out all feelings of criticism, too. If you think to yourself, "This person is really dumb," you may show it in your manner, defeating all you have been trying to accomplish.

Avoid Total Disagreement

If you want to become extremely unpopular, just speak out for the viewpoint opposite to the one being expressed. When you contradict the speaker, you are guilty of being rude. Even more unpleasant, however, you will usually stop the conversation dead. A mild response is much more effective, even if the speaker had made a foolish remark. "Do you really think so?" may sound spineless to you in such circumstances, but it is a better conversational tactic than a total contradiction, such as, "You are completely wrong!" Try to eliminate all feelings of competitiveness in conversation. There is no winner or loser; there should be, instead, a feeling of friendliness in a group talking together.

Don't Be Backward

If you are excessively shy, you may worry about yourself. Yet you may never have considered the effect of your shyness on others, for the backward conversationalist makes the others feel too forward. By fading into the background, you create an unnatural atmosphere that makes normal talkativeness seem excessive. Another difficulty with being overly shy is the tendency to appear cold and unfeeling to others. This makes people uncomfortable in your presence. Can you see how shyness, based on feelings of inferiority, will impress others as being based on self-centeredness? It is much better for you, and for the group in which you find yourself, to make an effort to be interested in others. If you start by showing interest in what others say, it won't be long before you will be able to say something, too.

Don't Hold Center Stage Too Long

If you tell a story, make it short. If you explain the way you think about something, hit the highlights only, leaving out the details. You must do this in order to leave space for others to talk, too. If you monopolize the conversation more than a moment or two, you will seem to be seeking the spotlight. This should be avoided, especially by the beginner in the art of conversation. When you are talking you are not listening.

Watch Your Eye Contact

A very important part of talking in a group is looking at all of the members of the group. This makes them feel included; again, it builds them up. If you look at just one person as you speak, the others will feel excluded. It is hard to tear your eyes away from someone who seems to be responding to you; but if you are to converse well, you must make an effort to do so. Try looking first to your left, then to your right, and then straight ahead. As you look in each direction, focus your eyes on some feature of one of the persons in that area. It *is* hard to look listeners directly in the eye; but make yourself do it. It's very important.

Watch Your Space

The distance or territory between you and your listener has an impact on how well you get your message across. For example, think of the reaction you would have if you were sitting in an empty bus, and a stranger sat next to you. Have you noticed how people react in a full elevator—they stand rigid and look at the indicator above the door or at the floor. This discomfort comes from encroachment on personal space. This happens also in conversation. If you violate someone's space by getting too close, they may instinctively back away and become uncomfortable. If this occurs, your message is lost and the conversation will soon terminate. The typical recommended space for casual conversation is one and one-half to two and one-half feet. We expect others to respect our space and we are expected to respect the territory of others. Our needs for space are culturally determined, and therefore what an American would consider acceptable conversational distance may be different from what a Japanese person or person from the Middle East would find acceptable.

Keep Your Statements Pleasant

When you first start developing your skill in conversation, you should avoid unpleasant topics, criticism of others, sarcasm, and pessimism. In fact, it would be a good idea to avoid them entirely. It is especially important, however, for the beginner to refrain from derogatory remarks. In the first place, few people admire the person who makes such remarks. In the second place, they destroy the spirit of friendship that is built up by good conversation.

Make Yourself Talk

The conversational beginner may have some trouble getting started. It is a good idea, therefore, to have some plan ready before you begin. You may decide to compliment one of the speakers; this is always a good approach. Just saying, "How interesting. I had never thought of that," is really praise of the other person's remarks. Or you can say, "Do you really think this will happen?" This is complimentary to the person speaking because it shows you are thinking about what has been said. Another opener for the beginner is a question. The speaker is always glad to have a question because this gives him or her the chance to talk to a definite point. If someone has been talking about a hobby, for example, you might ask, "How long did it take you to learn the technique?" A question is another sincere form of flattery. It is an easy way, too, to get a conversation started.

Avoid Laying Down the Law

A good conversationalist keeps a tolerant attitude. If you preach, if you hand down judgments, others will not enjoy listening to you. The secret is to keep an open mind. A conversation should be a free exchange of ideas. No one person should try to dominate it. Avoid, then, giving the final word on any subject. This will permit other persons in the group to add what they think. This is one way of keeping the conversational ball rolling.

WHAT TO SAY WHEN

Many of us have no difficulty carrying on a conversation after it has been started, but we do have some trouble starting it. Is there any rule to help get that first minute of conversation under way? Think for a moment of the most common subject of casual conversation, the weather. Why do strangers who must say something to each other resort to, "Is it hot enough for you?" It's a safe topic, that's why. The other person is certain to have something to say on the subject. When starting a conversation, then, it is best to begin with something about which everyone has an opinion.

When you use a question to begin a conversation, be careful to choose one that cannot be answered by a flat *yes* or *no*. Instead of the question asked in the previous paragraph, which would be almost sure to be answered, "Yes," you might say, "How long has it been since we had a good rainstorm?" This isn't any more sparkling than the previous question, but it does require some thought and a more or less complete sentence in reply. Asking a question that requires a statement in answer will keep the conversation going for a time, at least.

Some questions should be avoided. These include personal questions, particularly those involving health and money. If you are in doubt as to whether a question is too personal, put yourself in the other person's shoes. Would you like someone to ask you why your nose is red and your eyes all puffy? Would you like someone to ask how much you paid for the clothes you are wearing, or how much your car cost? It is also wise, when starting a conversation, to avoid emotionally tinged subjects, such as religion and politics.

Talking with Your Supervisors

Beginning workers are frequently ill at ease when talking with their supervisors. A good tip to remember is a single word: *follow*. In most cases, it is better to let the other person lead the conversation and listen more than you talk. If your supervisor is thinking or is deeply engrossed with something, it's best to avoid conversation except for important matters. On the other hand, if your supervisor is in a humorous mood, follow the lead—laugh at the jokes. Tell one yourself! If you are asked for your opinion on something, give it promptly, tactfully, and confidently. If you follow the other person's lead in all oral communication, if you develop the skill to

ILLUSTRATION 13-2.
When talking to super-
visors, follow their lead.

Richard Younker

pick up clues to feelings by paying attention to facial expressions, gestures, and so on, you will have no trouble. These clues are called **nonverbal communication.** They will often tell you more about a person's feelings than the spoken word. Review Chapter 8 for some additional points on how to communicate with your supervisor.

Talking with Workers under Your Supervision

When you are promoted to a supervisory position of any kind, such as supervisor, chief clerk, or executive assistant, the roles are reversed. Now it is important that you put your staff members at ease. Of course, the best way to put another person at ease is to feel relaxed yourself. Even when you have started up the ladder of success, you should still be yourself. You should not try to imitate the speech, the mannerisms, or the style of someone higher up the ladder than you are. Remember, too, the importance of a positive attitude toward those whose work you supervise. If you honestly like your staff members, they will know it. Your communication will be easier. In addition to feeling positively toward your staff members, you should tell them you appreciate their good work. Everyone needs recognition; give it when you can.

When it is necessary to make a comment about work that is not good, try the device of getting the worker to talk. Ask questions about the work. If your feeling is positive, if you have given praise when it is deserved, your task of constructive criticism will not be so difficult. Always remember, however, that criticism must be for the action, not for the person. You never say, "You must be really dumb not to follow these simple directions!"

Instead, you might say, "Did you understand the directions for making out the sales slips? If you did, I must ask you what happened with these slips that were filled out yesterday." Notice, in the latter example, that the slips become the villain—not the worker. This point is an important one. Avoid direct accusations. Saying *you* when you praise and not saying *you* when you give blame is a skill worth cultivating.

IMPROVING COMMUNICATION

As you communicate with others, you may either talk or listen. When you listen, you are the receiver. When you talk, you are the sender. The following aids to communication apply specifically to the activity of sending. You *send* the communication when you speak or write.

Be Specific

In either speaking or writing you will *send* more effectively if you deal in specifics, if you avoid generalities. General statements are uninteresting mainly because they are hard to picture in your mind. Writing or speaking about a college, for example, you might picture a red brick building covered with ivy and think "Central College." Using the words "Central College," the person reading or listening to your message would probably get the same mental picture. What will your reader or listener picture, however, if you write or say "college"? The words "Yale University" may appear in the mental picture. The word "college" is not as concrete as the name of the specific college. If you write or say "school," you are still more abstract, since your reader or listener may visualize an elementary school. If you write or say "institution," you climb to still another level of abstraction, since your reader or listener may now visualize a hospital or even a jail.

The way to avoid abstract words is to ask yourself one or more of the five W's—who, where, when, why (or how), and what. If you are tempted to say "charitable organization," you would ask yourself, "What charitable organization?" and your answer might be the Red Cross. The listener certainly would get a clearer picture from the words Red Cross than from "charitable organization."

Be Clear

When you communicate clearly, the reader or listener gets the message you send. Your message will be received correctly only if you make your statement or request so clear that it cannot be misunderstood. Following are three devices that can be recommended with confidence to help you speak or write clearly.

Brevity.   The reader or listener will understand five words better than ten words. Ten will be better understood than twenty. In the same way, a two-syllable word will be better understood than a six-syllable word. A paragraph containing six lines will be easier to understand than one containing twelve lines. Brevity must not be overdone, of course, since your communication must be grammatically correct and appropriately phrased. Within these limits, though, your communication will be clearer if you use short words, short sentences, and short paragraphs.

Variety.   Your communication will get attention if you avoid sameness, such as several sentences beginning the same way. Another way to put variety into what you say or write is to avoid using the same words or phrases over and over. Avoid using trite and meaningless phrases like "you know," "in terms of," and "at this point in time." Watch, too, a tendency to write several sentences in succession that all start the same way, as well as that of having all of your sentences the same length. Interest and clarity will be improved if you have variety in the way you make up your sentences.

Itemization.   Clarity is improved if you itemize any sort of list that you wish to communicate. Notice how hard it is to understand the following written instructions: "Please go to the records management department and locate the letter written by R.J. Blezek last Tuesday, and then make two copies and send one of them to the auditing department and the other one to the accounting department, and to the one to the accounting department attach a copy of the contract signed by Blezek in November of last year."

By itemizing these instructions, we improve their clarity, as follows: "Please (1) make two copies of the letter sent to R.J. Blezek on Tuesday, October 6; (2) make a copy of the contract signed by R.J. Blezek in November of last year; (3) send one copy of the letter and a copy of the con-tract to the accounting department; and (4) send the other copy of the letter to the auditing department."

The instructions are even easier if the writer lists the items one below the other as follows:

Will you please take care of the following:

1. Make two copies of the letter to R.J. Blezek on October 6 of this year.

2. Make a copy of the Blezek contract signed in November of last year.
3. Send one copy of the letter and a copy of the contract to the accounting department.
4. Send the other copy of the letter to the auditing department.

Be Positive

You have learned how important it is to be positive in earlier chapters. As you will see, it is just as important to write or to take care of business matters over the telephone in a positive manner. In other words, it is better to say what you *can* do instead of what you *cannot* do. When you must say, "No," however, one of the following ways will help you.

Imply the Negative. If someone asks you, as manager of a mail order company, for copies of your sales letters, you might answer, "Since our company depends wholly on sales and collection letters for its business, they are for our use only." Such an answer strongly *implies* that the answer is "No," yet it does not actually say "No."

Say What You Can Do. Another device for handling negatives is to avoid the "No" by saying what you can do. For example, a customer may call you to ask if a Christmas order can be moved forward and shipped on December 1. Instead of answering that early shipment is impossible, you might say, "We'll have your order to you by December 15—with seven shopping days still remaining before Christmas."

Use Sentence Structure. If you must say "No," the sting can be removed somewhat by putting the "No" in the dependent clause of the sentence, the part of the sentence that cannot stand alone. Instead of saying, "You failed to send the catalog number of the camera you wanted," you would say, "If you will give me the catalog number of your camera, I'll send it right out."

Impersonalize the Negative. Your "No" answer will be more acceptable if a *thing* (rather than the person) is the subject of your sentence. By saying "This tire appears to have failed on the sidewall," the listener will accept your statement. But if you say, "What did you do—run this tire into a curb?" your statement sounds accusing and your listener will not accept it. Still another way to impersonalize the negative is to put the listener or reader in a group. To get a newly employed TV service technician always to check a particular circuit, it could be stated in the following way: "Our service people have found that, if you always check this circuit first, you can save a lot of time when troubleshooting the loss of video." Such a statement would encourage the new person to follow the correct procedure without being harsh.

SPEAKING BEFORE GROUPS

If you are asked to speak to a group—a committee, a club, a staff, an organization—your procedure will be similar to that used in writing. You collect your thoughts in written form, organize them, and write and rewrite your outline. But there is a difference. When you prepare a talk, it is usually best to stop at the outline stage. Some good speakers, it is true, write down their speeches and memorize them. But those who speak frequently seem to do better if they first outline their thoughts carefully and then speak from

ILLUSTRATION 13-3. Those who speak frequently do better when they carefully outline their thoughts, and then speak from the outline.

the outline. One reason for this is that effective reading is even more difficult than effective speaking. Unless you have been trained in reading aloud, you will give a dull and uninteresting presentation if you rely on reading alone. If you are a "just starting" speaker, the following tips may be helpful.

Notes for Speaking

Type or print your notes on index cards instead of on regular sheets of paper. Cards can be handled so that the audience is less likely to be distracted by them. Don't be concerned about the audience being aware of your cards—the cards signal to them that you are *prepared*. If you use stories, dramatic statistics, or other examples (and they are good to use), type them on colored cards of the same size. The use of colored cards signals the fact that the example is coming up and helps you prepare for a change of pace or approach in your presentation. It is also a good idea to write on the back of each example card the date and title of the talk in which it was used. This technique will help you avoid using the same example before the same group another time.

Tips for Improving Your Speaking

To improve your speaking ability, two attributes are needed: relaxation and practice.

Relaxation. Learn to relax your throat. Yawn. Notice how your throat feels. When you yawn, your throat is open. Try to keep this feeling when you are speaking. If you learn to relax, you will benefit in another way. That same sense of relaxation will be conveyed to your audience, helping them to listen more easily.

Practice. Take advantage of every opportunity you have to talk with others. *Want* to share, to communicate. Next, listen to a recording of your voice. You may not recognize what you hear as belonging to you, but you will probably note certain faults that you can improve. Some possible faults are these:

1. Do you project your voice? If you want to be a good speaker, you must "push" your voice to the person farthest away from you. Learn to speak directly to the ones in the back row.
2. Do you speak with your best pitch? There is a simple test for finding your best pitch. Go to a piano and sing "ah" down the

scale to your lowest comfortable pitch. Then sing back up four whole notes. This level is your best speaking pitch. Most of us speak with a higher pitch than is pleasing.

3. Does your voice sound alive? If you are interested and enthusiastic about what you are saying, you will be interesting—and your voice will sound vibrant and alive.

4. Do you speak your words clearly? Speaking clearly results in proper articulation. This quality is improved if you pronounce your consonants sharply.

5. Do you look at your audience? Your listeners will be much more interested in what you have to say if you look directly at them. Looking at your audience is called "eye contact." It means that you look at someone's face in the center of your audience for a short time, then at someone's face on one side of your audience, then at someone's face on the other side. Never devote all your attention to just one part of your audience, since this makes those in the other areas feel left out (and they will tune *you* out). Also remember that looking at the walls above their heads will not do. And *never* look out of the window while you are speaking.

Do You Use Space Fillers? The nervous speaker punctuates remarks with "uh," "ah," and "er." To break the "uh-ah-er" habit, in addition to relaxing, you should just stop speaking when you are at a loss for words. Pause, look pleasant, and no one will know the difference. In fact, a pause is actually helpful, since many of us speak too fast. Silence is acceptable. Silence may be used to emphasize a point as well as provide you with a few seconds to regroup your thoughts.

Another bad conversational habit is the excessive use of "you know" or "y'know." By continually using "y'know" in your conversation, you may cause the listener to quit listening. After all, if the listener already knows what you are saying, then why listen? "Do you know?" is an honest question. "Y'know" is a bad habit.

QUESTIONS AND PROJECTS

1. It is Monday morning and you arrive at your workplace knowing that a new coworker, Susan Jaderstrom, will be spending her first day on the

job. You meet Susan at the time clock. What are some lead sentences that you might use to start a conversation with her and assist her in feeling comfortable in the new setting?

2. How would you start a conversation with the following people?

   a. your supervisor
   b. a person who works in your building that you have not met
   c. a prospective customer
   d. a union steward

3. Prepare a list of trite expressions that you hear often. You may want to work with others in the preparation of this list. On the opposite side of the page list expressions or phrases that could replace the trite phrases. The following will get you started: "smooth as silk," "busy as a bee," "quiet as a mouse," "tough as nails," and "pale as a ghost."

4. Prepare note cards for a speech on how to start a conversation with a coworker. Use the information in this chapter to help you prepare the note cards.

5. Listen to your favorite news commentator and bring to class a list of colorful words and phrases used or words pronounced differently from the way you are accustomed to hearing them.

6. Reread the first four suggestions for eliminating faults in your speaking: (Do you project your voice? Do you speak with your best pitch? Does your voice sound alive? Do you speak your words clearly?) For one week spend ten or fifteen minutes a day on *one* fault that is most serious for you. For example, if you lack projection, count from one to ten aloud, starting softly on one and increasing your projection until it is at its strongest point on the count of ten.

7. To increase your vocabulary, try the following plan of learning a new word each week.

   a. Choose a word from your daily reading that you do not know.
   b. Place this word, including pronunciation and meaning, on your bulletin board or chalkboard or attach it to your mirror, where you will see it several times a day.
   c. Involve your family or friends in the activity.
   d. Use the new word in your speaking; perhaps others will use the word, too.
   e. Remember: Each week choose a new word—but don't forget the new words you learned earlier. Keep a list of all the words you have worked on, and make them a part of your daily speech.

CASE PROBLEMS

1.   The Customer Is Always Right.

Louis Welti works in the office of the sales department of a coffee company. He keeps the records of the salespeople who are on the city routes. His books show the supplies the salespeople take out of stock and their returns in cash and merchandise. Louis is exceptionally efficient. If there is a mistake in the record of a route person, Louis always catches it. If there is an argument about reports, Louis can offer the needed facts to eliminate further confusion. Louis does have one fault; he has not developed a courteous telephone technique. The manager has had a number of complaints from customers who are annoyed at the way Louis handles situations over the telephone. The following are typical of Louis's conversations:

An irate customer says, ''I told the salesperson I wanted a light roast and I got a package of dark roast instead.'' Louis answers, ''Why don't you give the dark roast a try? It's one of our best sellers.''

A dissatisfied customer says, ''I just received my bill and you have charged me $10.16 for Saturday, November 18. I did not place or receive an order on that date.'' Louis says, ''You must be mistaken. The bills are checked most carefully before we send them out.''

An angry customer says, ''I asked that my orders be delivered on Saturday morning, and this is the third time they have been sent out on Monday.'' Louis says, ''This is the first time I have heard about it. Are you sure you told the delivery clerk?''

When the office manager speaks to Louis about the complaints he has received, Louis defends himself vigorously. He knows he is right; he says he is positive the customers are mistaken. The next time, the office manager comes to the rescue to keep a battle from developing and resolves to tell Louis what he should have said in each of the cases cited.

a.   Assuming that you are the office manager, how would you have answered each of the three customers?

b.   Why does Louis talk as he does? Do you think he may be covering up a lack of confidence?

c.   What personal techniques should Louis develop in addition to keeping records?

2.   What about English Mechanics?

Barbara Chamberlain works for a construction company. In her letters, she is very careless about her English usage. Such matters as grammar and old-fashioned phrasing seem of no importance to her. George Madsen, a young man who works in the office under Barbara's supervision, has always done well in English courses in school. He has also done quite well in a course in business communication.

    a.   Should George do anything about this situation?

    b.   Should Barbara be expected to learn and use better English skills?

    c.   If George decides to correct the mistakes in grammar, how far should he go in changing his supervisor's style or characteristic way of expressing her meaning?

Your Standards of Conduct

LEARNING OBJECTIVES:

1. Explain the value and importance of a personal reputation for moral behavior.

2. Explain the meaning of larceny and identify a variety of typical examples of "borderline" dishonesty.

3. Recognize and avoid various forms of expense account abuse.

4. Identify various kinds of perquisites and bribery, and exercise good judgment in taking advantage of them.

5. Demonstrate dedication and loyalty to your employer.

6. Maintain a high standard of sexual morality and avoid drugs and alcohol.

> Oliver had applied for a position as a technical writer for a firm that produces computer software. In the routine check with former employers, Mr. Jackson, the personnel director, discovered that seven years earlier Oliver had lost his job as a salesperson. The former supervisor said, ''We had to let Oliver go because of a slight indiscretion on his part.'' In fact, the ''indiscretion'' was unauthorized long-distance telephone calls

> on the company phone. In conversation with the person who
> would be Oliver's supervisor, Mr. Jackson said, "Oliver has ex-
> cellent references from his recent employers, and he is a talented
> writer. We could certainly use him. Do you think we should rule
> him out because of whatever he did seven years ago?"

___ *When* you have been employed for a length of time, you will be aware that there is no accepted set of rules for behavior in the world of work. You will work with a cross section of people. Some will have an "anything goes" standard of conduct; others will be strict in their views of what should and should not be done. It is up to you to set moral standards for yourself. Therefore, you should judge carefully as you develop your own "rules and regulations." Your morality—your integrity—will be defined by how well you conform to the standards of what you personally believe to be right. However, you also must recognize that your standards may not exactly match those of your employers and coworkers. What they believe to be right will also be an important consideration as you make the day-to-day decisions regarding your conduct. Obviously, if you violate the standards and expectations of your employers and coworkers, you face the possibility of negative consequences. In this chapter we consider some of the typical situations in which you may find yourself making moral judgments regarding your own behavior.

YOUR REPUTATION: A VALUABLE ASSET

Many people are concerned by a lack of ethics and morality in business. Because business is concerned with profits, because it is competitive, and because success is based on rivalry, some will argue that business cannot be moral.

An ambitious businessperson, however, must look beyond the surface evidence and study the long-range results of morality in business. This survey will reveal that companies that have become firmly established through years of service are more interested in protecting their good reputation than in making a single sale or in making quick profits. Young firms that want to establish lasting goodwill are more interested in their integrity than in the profit of the moment. In testing the effect of morality, take a hard look at the businesses that have successfully stood the test of time.

ILLUSTRATION 14–1.
When you have developed
a reputation for being
dedicated, loyal, honest
and conscientious, doors
of opportunity will open
for you.

As a businessperson you should guard your record of morality because it is a valuable possession. You should guard it because you are ethical and have faith, a sense of fair play, and a social conscience. You should guard it for selfish reasons, too, because it is as valuable to you in business as capital or education.

Successful businesspeople should also be interested, not in a moment of glory and success, but in long-range respect. Seldom are there any secrets in business. Even long after an incident of immorality, someone will remember. Facts can come to light in other ways, too, for there are many types of records. That a person did not make a sale, that a task was poorly completed, that an employee was promoted will probably be forgotten. But immorality will become a part of the record. If this record is not in writing, it will be whispered.

On many details of morality people do not agree, but some basic principles are common to the consciences of all people. Other basic principles, in addition to those of all society, are recognized by businesspeople.

Success-related personality factors, as indicated earlier, are dedication, loyalty, honesty, and conscientiousness. These personal qualities are highly prized by employers. Therefore, your success in the world of work depends on the impression your employers have about your standards of conduct.

Just as a business firm has an image to develop and protect, so you must develop and protect your personal image. The following sections will focus on some of the typical situations in which you may build up or tear down that image. You will see that there are many opportunities to build up or tear down—many choices to make. These choices will challenge your integrity and strength of character. Sometimes there is a high price to pay when you live up to your own standards of conduct. But after you have developed a reputation for being dedicated, loyal, honest, and conscientious, that reputation will pay off. Doors of opportunity will open for you. Employers will give you preference in hiring. They will reward you with advancement and greater responsibility. On the other hand, if you should develop a reputation for being less than conscientious, inclined to dishonesty, or lacking in loyalty, doors of opportunity will remain closed. You should expect employers to take this image into consideration. Advancement and increased responsibility will pass you by. In the long run, a bad reputation can be a heavy burden to carry.

THE MANY FACES OF DISHONESTY

Seldom, if ever, can you expect to find a totally honest person. Employers do not expect that. They do not expect absolute dedication, loyalty, or conscientious effort under all conditions. Therefore, when a supervisor writes a letter of recommendation saying, "Lou is an honest person," the message is that Lou, in comparison with other workers, is more honest than most. Under extreme stress almost anyone may be expected to behave with less than absolute honesty. But the person with high standards of honesty will be able to resist great pressure and remain honest. Your challenge is to set standards of honesty for yourself which will cause your employers to admire and respect you—to expect what they consider to be a satisfactory level of honesty in your dealings with them.

Rather than present a list of rules for honesty in employment, some situations will be presented which might challenge your own honesty. As the possible alternatives to the situation are discussed, you will begin to understand what honesty means in the world of work. Rather than simply trying to set standards of honesty for you, this will help you see what typical employers might expect of employees with reputations for being honest. Then you should be able to measure your own personal standards against those of your future employers. Hopefully you will want to set high standards of honesty for yourself. In the long run, your honesty will be rewarded.

Pat and Jan were sharing a hero sandwich at the deli where they often meet for lunch. "I'm amazed at what some people get away with in the hardware business," said Jan. "If you want to, you can get away with anything." "It's the same at our bank. But you could find yourself unemployed—maybe in jail," Pat responded. "I'm not talking about crime," Jan said. "I mean things like writing letters on company time, using the postage meter for personal mail, taking extra time at the water cooler, showing favoritism to customers who bribe you with Christmas gifts, not reporting cash transactions to avoid income tax. I could go on and on—and they get away with it!" There was a pause. Then Pat said "You know, Jan, we don't have to pay for this sandwich. Or do we?"

Larceny

Larceny, by definition, means to take something fully intending not to return the thing to its owner. Larceny is theft and a larcenist is a thief. But any judge will tell you that many convicted larcenists do not think of themselves as criminals. For example, you may know someone who has taken merchandise from a store without paying for it. But do you think of your acquaintances who have been guilty of shoplifting as criminals? (Yes, larceny is, legally, a criminal offense.)

There are many kinds of larceny in the workplace. Grand larceny is the legal term for stealing something of great value (over a legally specified amount). Petty larceny describes the theft of something of little value. The legal penalties are greater for grand larceny, but petty larceny is probably a greater problem for employers. Shoplifting by the employees in a retail business is only one form of the problem, however. Employee theft of supplies, equipment, and materials is another form of petty theft which causes employers great concern.

Most businessowners and managers will say privately that they expect some petty theft by employees, just as retailers expect a certain amount of shoplifting to occur. But not all employers use the same strategies for eliminating employee theft. A few assume that they can make the consequences so harsh that no one will dare to steal anything. They may press legal charges in court, possibly spending far more money than the cost of the stolen items. This helps to dramatize and publicize the fact that the management considers petty theft to be a serious offense. More often, however, the offender will be fired on the spot. The employer may assume that the damage to the employee's reputation is punishment enough. And, indeed, it may be.

Suppose, for a moment, you had been convicted of petty theft. Think of how you might feel as you face an employment interviewer. How can you soften the effect of the petty larceny conviction on your employment record? On the positive side, think of how you might feel having a spotless employment record, knowing your previous employer has, in a letter of recommendation, described you as a completely honest person—one who can be trusted. You have never been known to take anything, not even a postage stamp or a paper clip, for personal use.

Knowing what is acceptable behavior and what is not, as your employer sees it, is not always easy. Following are some examples of behavior that some employers may allow. Others may consider such behavior to be dishonest.

> Taking small quantities of inexpensive office supplies such as pencils, file folders, and transparent tape

> Sending personal mail on company stationery, using company postage, and using company long-distance telephone lines for personal calls

> Taking supplies or materials that the company produces or uses in large quantities

> Taking things that the employer has no use for and wants to dispose of such as day-old bakery goods, used packing boxes, surplus or waste building materials, defective or damaged merchandise, scrap paper, and free samples of merchandise or supplies

What you must do to protect your reputation for honesty is find out what your employer's expectations are and be sure your standards of conduct conform to those expectations. You can learn about what is expected by simply asking, "Terry, do you mind if I take a pickup truck load of sand to fill the sandbox I made for my cousin?" Or you might be less direct, "Dan, may I use the company long-distance line to call my parents in Minneapolis, or should I have the call billed to my home phone?"

You may also learn what is acceptable and what is not by observing and talking with your coworkers. But be careful. You may find yourself—along with others—violating your employer's rules. An example of this occurred in a large construction firm in a western state. Jane noticed several of her coworkers taking company-supplied flashlight batteries in their lunch pails. When she asked if she could take some for her own use, a veteran worker replied, "Sure, we take a few batteries for deer hunting every year. Help yourself." Jane took six batteries, three in each coat pocket. The office manager happened to notice the bulging pockets. Jane's explanation that, "Everyone else is doing it and they told me it was OK," was not very convincing. Fortunately, Jane was only reprimanded. But company officials investigated and found a 200 percent increase in the use of flashlight batteries—always just before deer hunting season.

Expense Account Abuse

Many business occupations involve travel, meals, and lodging at company expense. Selling "on the road," traveling to deliver merchandise or to service customers' equipment, and participating in business conferences are cases in point. Some companies have liberal expense accounting policies. They trust the employee to keep personal records and simply report what was spent. Other employers enforce elaborate rules and regulations with lots of paperwork. These detailed rules and recordkeeping procedures are designed to protect the employer from employees who might use the expense accounting system to obtain extra income. Here are some examples of petty theft by using expense account loopholes.

Reporting more expensive meals than actually eaten

Asking reimbursement for meals not paid for (such as those received on an airplane)

Including liquor (reported as food) on expense accounts

Reporting greater automobile mileage than actually driven

Riding the bus but reporting taxi fares

Asking for full reimbursement when two people share a ride

Staying in exclusive hotels, traveling first-class, or eating at the most expensive restaurants

Asking reimbursement for expenses for vacation time (taking an extra day for recreation at the end of a business trip)

Including personal long-distance telephone calls on a hotel bill

Some of these practices are clearly dishonest and unacceptable. Some appear to be questionable. Others may seem, to most people, to be perfectly

ILLUSTRATION 14−2.   Expense accounts are often provided to employees who must travel on business. Inexperienced workers must learn how to use expense accounting in a way that strengthens their reputation for honesty.

acceptable. Your challenge, as always, is to learn what your employer expects of you in a given situation. Then you must avoid abuses that can damage your reputation for honesty.

As an inexperienced worker, you will need to make a special effort to learn "how the game is played." But be aware that you may encounter individuals who will set a bad example—"bending the rules" or cheating whenever and however they can. At the opposite extreme, you will find individuals who live by very high moral standards. For instance, they stay with friends or relatives and pass the savings in hotel bills along to the employer. Or they may take advantage of the lowest possible air fare and travel at an inconvenient time to get a lower-priced ticket. They may eat inexpensive meals, carry bag lunches, and in other ways conserve on food expenses. In one unusual case, a sales representative was found to be reporting unusually low travel expenses. When the expense account auditor investigated, it was found that the representative owned a small car which used very little gasoline. Making sure the reimbursement only covered actual expenses, the representative was reporting less than the actual mileage.

When you find someone behaving this way, chances are it will be the boss. The owner or manager of a business knows that lower expenses mean higher profits. When you get the profits, your motivation to economize is increased. But you should realize that in the long run both you and your employer will benefit when you help your employer make a profit. And just as there are people who use the expense account to steal from their employers, there are people who use it to conserve and reduce expenses for their employers. Probably you will find most of your coworkers' actions to be somewhere between these extremes. The majority of people are honest in reporting their actual expenses; they lose or gain very little.

To conclude this discussion of expense accounts, consider this: When employees' personal standards of honesty are high, a relaxed, trusting relationship grows. Employers seldom question or even review the expense accounts reported by trusted employees. When necessary, the employees can report unusually high expenses without hesitation. It is a pleasure to work in such an atmosphere. But it is far from pleasant to work in an atmosphere of insecurity and mistrust that results when employers see expense accounting as a potential tool for petty larceny by their employees.

Perquisites

A **perquisite** is defined as a privilege, gain, or profit incidental to regular salary or wages, especially one expected or promised. As this definition shows, there are many perquisites that have nothing to do with a person's moral standards. For example, Norman works at a restaurant. He gets an hourly wage plus tips. He also gets free meals for himself and a 50 percent discount on food he or anyone in his family buys.

For every perquisite, there is usually an opportunity for some kind of abuse. In our example, Norman may decide to have a party. His employer probably would be upset to see that Norman used his food discount privilege to buy forty dollars worth of fried chicken for twenty dollars. Or Norman may get into a habit of ordering the most expensive steak sandwich just at closing time and taking most of it home supposedly for his dog—or worse—leaving it on his plate.

Another challenge to Norman's integrity is how he manages his tips. He may occasionally pick up tips intended for a coworker. He may hold some money back for himself when tips are to be shared with other employees. He may record only part of his tips to avoid paying income tax on the unreported earnings.

Almost any job you can think of has certain perquisites, and almost every perquisite offers some opportunity for exploitation—or dishonesty. Consider the following situations.

1. Many retail stores offer employee discounts on merchandise.
2. Employees of a small midwestern meat-packing plant (including office workers) may buy veal tenderloin at one-third of the market price.
3. Employees of a large automotive service station are allowed to take any parts that may be discarded when repairs are made.
4. Many automobile and motorcycle dealers allow their employees to drive used vehicles that are in stock. (Some dealers allow employees to drive customers' vehicles!)
5. An office machines company gives high school business teachers first choice in the purchase of typewriters that have been traded in—for a small fraction of the market value.
6. A television dealer allows service department employees to work on their own sets, evenings and weekends, with parts provided at the dealer's cost.

These are only a few examples. You probably could think of many more. Also, you could probably imagine many different ways to take advantage of such situations to an employer's disadvantage. This is where your good judgment, your sense of fair play, and your basic honesty will guide you.

Bribery

When you first think of "bribery" as a form of employee dishonesty, you will probably be reminded of gambling, political pressure, and white collar crime involving business executives. But bribery, on a small scale, may occur at any level in a business enterprise.

Here is a different example of a form of bribery that you may encounter. Lee, a salesclerk in a pharmacy, often chooses the brand of a product for the customer. In this instance four brands of cold medicine, all having the same formula, were on display. Whenever a customer asked for cold medicine without specifying a brand, the salesclerks would make the choice themselves. One drug wholesaler found a way to encourage salesclerks to give preference to Brand X when selecting cold medicine for a customer.

This is how the scheme worked. A removable sticker, about the size of a postage stamp, was placed on every package of Brand X. When the drug firm representative made regular visits to a pharmacy, all the stickers each salesclerk had collected would be redeemed at fifteen cents each. Lee was able to earn about fifteen dollars in cash per week this way over and above regular wages. The drug wholesaler did not refer to the payoff money as bribery, however. A more socially acceptable name was needed for it. So the wholesaler chose to refer to the small bribes as perquisites and every salesclerk was given a little box with the word "perks" printed on it.

Of course, being in a position to benefit from petty bribery is a perquisite if you take advantage of it. And many people would not consider it wrong for a salesclerk to accept the "perks" described above. Eventually, in court, a Brand X competitor was able to show that the scheme was illegal. Only the Brand X drug wholesaler was punished. But were the salespeople partly at fault? Were the pharmacy managers at fault when they permitted the petty bribery to occur? Does the fact that some stores did not allow their employees to accept the "perks" affect your opinion?

Perquisites are more often associated with high-level executive positions. Some examples are reserved parking spaces, country club memberships, stock purchase options, and the use of company cars. One linen supply company executive arranged for the company to provide two cars. One was used for travel on company business. The other was supposed to be used by the maintenance supervisor. However, all the maintenance workers were employed at one plant. Because the maintenance supervisor never used the

ILLUSTRATION 14-3.   Perquisites are more often associated with high level executive positions.

car, the executive's children used it and chose a new car every year at company expense.

These cases illustrate how petty bribery and the abuse of special privileges can occur in the world of work. Following are a few other examples. In each instance you will see the same pattern:

1. Gordon collects tickets at a movie theater
2. Pablo, Sue, and Mary Ann go to a movie. Gordon accepts two tickets for three people.
3. After the show, Gordon joins Mary Ann to make it a double date.

1. The purchasing manager has responsibility for obtaining supplies for the hospital.
2. The surgical supplies salesperson wants to sell bandages to the hospital.
3. On Saturday the purchasing manager and the surgical supplies salesperson play two rounds of golf (paid for on the salesperson's expense account). On Monday the hospital places an order with the surgical supplies salesperson.

1. The receptionist schedules appointments with the executive. (Appointments with the executive are valuable.)
2. The client (a seafood wholesaler) is willing to pay the receptionist for scheduling appointments for her ahead of other clients.
3. At Christmas time the client gives the receptionist fifteen pounds of frozen lobster—as a present. (Actually, both individuals understand that the lobster is given in return for favoritism in scheduling appointments with the executive. There is no written or spoken contract. But a deal is made.)

1. The store display specialist has construction skills and materials available to her. (Also, she loves lobster.)
2. The receptionist wants a planter for her office. (She has fifteen pounds of frozen lobster.)
3. The display specialist builds a planter for the receptionist's office using company time and materials. She gets fifteen pounds of frozen lobster—as a gift.

At the opposite extreme are employers who assume that anyone associated with the company must live by certain moral and personal behavior standards. Examples are when the person is employed by a church, local government, or a school or community organization that has a public image to protect. Such employers have been known to fire a person for having been seen near or in an establishment deemed inappropriate.

THE DEDICATED WORKER

Thus far in this chapter you have explored what it means to develop your reputation for honesty. Now consider what it means for your reputation to be dedicated and loyal.

Just as honesty is a personality trait that shapes your behavior when you are tempted to be dishonest, dedication is also a part of your personality. A dedicated employee is likely to exhibit several positive attitudes, including loyalty and being conscientious. Your dedication will show in your standard of conduct when you face such opportunities (and temptations) as the following:

To do your own thing on company time

To put down coworkers as you climb the ladder of success

To gossip about your employer

To get even when you feel mistreated by your employer

To keep quiet when you know customers or coworkers are taking advantage of your employer

To allow social conversations with coworkers to interfere with getting the job done

To allow the use of alcohol or drugs to influence your job performance

When you accept a job and an employer accepts you as a worker, a contract is made. You agree to work. The employer agrees to pay you for your work. But there is more to the contract. You expect to be allowed to learn and progress on the job. You expect good supervision and training. You expect the employer to be honest with you—and fair. You expect a reasonably safe, pleasant place to work. You expect to have occasional rest periods, time for lunch, extra pay for overtime work, and other fringe benefits.

This is a very substantial list of expectations. But you are not entitled to any of them without meeting an equally substantial list of employer expectations. Many of those expectations are highlighted throughout this book—a positive attitude, productive work habits, initiative and motivation, knowledge and skills, and many more.

Among the most important of the typical employer's expectations is loyalty. Many employers complain that the young people of today are more likely to be disloyal than those of an earlier generation. This attitude is shown by some employers in their preference for hiring and promoting older workers. Of course, age and physical maturity do not automatically mean that the worker will be more mature in job performance and attitudes. But as a young worker, you will have to prove yourself. And your employer's expectations with respect to loyalty are most important.

Most employers are very intolerant of what they consider to be disloyal behavior. To help you understand what loyalty means to most employers, try to put yourself in the employer's position. Ask yourself, "How would I feel about this situation if I were the owner or manager of this business?"

Here is one example of how employee loyalty can be tested. Bill, as a waiter-trainee in a restaurant, noticed that some of the waiters and waitresses were receiving consistently larger tips than he was. Finally, he discovered the reason for it. Sandy, the person assigned to help train Bill, explained it this way. "What it amounts to is giving free drinks and salads," she said.

"You refill soft drink glasses but forget to add the extra drinks to the check. You serve salads that were not ordered, and tell the customers that it is on the house. Sometimes you just sort of forget to put drinks or salads on the check. Most often what they should have paid for the salads and drinks shows up in your tip."

Now Bill found himself in a dilemma—a situation where one way or the other he was bound to create a problem for himself. Should he report this practice to his supervisor or should he go along with the scheme? As it turned out, Bill chose loyalty to the employer over loyalty to his dishonest coworkers. When Bill left his job to return to college, the manager expressed appreciation for his loyalty. Also, Bill was promised a job at any future time and a good recommendation to any other prospective employer.

SEX, DRUGS, AND ALCOHOL ABUSE

You may be the type of individual who lives by the highest standard of sexual morality and a person who never drinks alcohol or abuses drugs. If so, these standards of conduct will probably be an asset as you seek employment and advancement in the world of work. As with the other personality traits discussed in this chapter, employers have a variety of expectations. Basically, you will find employers having one of the following three points of view.

At one extreme is the employer who cares only about one thing—production. In this situation no one will be overly concerned about what you do when you are not on the job. Your private life is your own business, as far as your employer is concerned. Whatever you are privately, your employer will only be concerned with how well you do the job you were hired to do. You will be expected to keep your personal life and affairs in control so they have no effect on your work.

At the opposite extreme are employers who assume that anyone associa-associated with the company must live by certain moral and personal behavior standards. Examples are when the person is employed by a church, local government, or a school or community organization that has a public image to protect. Such employers have been known to fire a person for having been seen near or in an establishment deemed inappropriate.

Between the two extremes described above are the employers who expect, like the first type of employer, that personal problems at home, drugs, and alcohol abuse will not influence job performance. But in addition, they may want to maintain a favorable company image. For example, a bank, a retail store, or a real estate agency might feel that their business would be hurt if customers think the company's salespeople are not of the highest moral character. This point of view is especially common in small communities (where company employees are recognized by everyone—and where stories of improper behavior get around quickly). Some of these employers may actually try to help their workers with company-sponsored programs. These programs may provide services such as counselors and doctors who can help with alcoholism and family problems.

In conclusion, remember that the higher your standards, the more options you have. You will have a wider selection of prospective employers. You will adapt and find acceptance in a greater variety of employment situations. You may find it difficult, at times, to maintain higher standards of conduct. But once you do, you will have good reason to take pride in yourself. Your chances for success and personal satisfaction will be increased. In the long run, you will be the winner.

QUESTIONS AND PROJECTS

1. How might you, as a beginning worker, learn the unwritten code of behavior that prevails in your workplace?

2. Are there any situations in which an "alibi" is better than the candid truth? Discuss this question.

3. You have heard it said that honesty is the best policy. Yet we find many examples of successful businessowners and managers who are accused of dishonesty—in advertising, selling methods, failing to stand behind what they sell, and so on. Is honesty the best policy in business today? In your opinion, why or why not?

4. Is it better to admit your mistakes or to try to cover them up? Under what kinds of circumstances might you want to make it appear that someone else is (at least partly) to blame? In a group discussion, share your experiences to determine what the likely consequences are when you cover up and when you tell all.

CASE PROBLEMS

1. To Draw or Not to Draw.

Tim is working part-time in the drafting department of a small manufacturing firm. Since he has access to graphic supplies, materials and equipment, he decides to use his coffee breaks and lunch periods to design and produce detailed sketches of a family room remodeling project for his home.

a. Should Tim ask permission or should he feel free to go ahead with the project, since he intends to do it on his own time?
b. How do you think his supervisor should respond if Tim asks permission?
c. What reasons might be given to justify refusing Tim's request?

2. The Encounter.

Hal worked the late night shift as an admitting clerk in a hospital. About 3:00 a.m. he heard a noise in the pharmacy. He opened the door and saw Mr. Swann, the hospital administrator, with a beaker of clear liquid in his hand. Mr. Swann said nothing when he saw Hal. He simply set the beaker on the counter, walked past Hal and out the door. Hal checked the beaker and found it to contain alcohol. Thinking it was none of his business, and fearing that he might be fired if he said anything, Hal said nothing to anyone about the incident. Two months later Mr. Swann was replaced as administrator, with no explanation. But everyone on the hospital staff figured out the reason when Hal admitted Mr. Swann to the hospital later as an emergency case—for alcohol poisoning.

a. Did Hal make the right choice in keeping quiet about the incident? If not, what should Hal have done?
b. If Mr. Swann had caught Hal in the pharmacy with a beaker of alcohol, would he have overlooked the incident? If not, should he have overlooked it?

3.   Out the Back Door and in the Front.

Assume you have discovered that some of the employees in the supermarket where you work are stealing empty soft drink containers and selling them to youngsters in the neighborhood at half their value. You see some of these children selling the same bottles at the checkstand of your store.

   a.   What are your responsibilities to your employer? to your coworkers?
   b.   What should the store manager do upon discovering the details of this situation?

4.   No Personal Calls.

Ruth McDonald is busy with her work when she receives a personal telephone call from her friend, Harry, who wants to find out about a weekend trip that is being planned. Harry is working at his first job; Ruth knows Harry does not realize that the office is no place for personal calls. Ruth doesn't want to hurt Harry's feelings, so she tries to be tactful. Finally, she says, ''Harry I must go now. Mrs. Maxwell is buzzing me. See you Friday.''

   a.   Do you think Harry was made aware that he should not call Ruth during office hours?
   b.   Should Ruth have been more honest with Harry so he would understand how to behave in the future?
   c.   Can you think of a tactful way that Ruth could have informed Harry of the general rule regarding personal telephone calls during business hours?

5.   Business within a Business.

Bertha works as an assembler in a sash and door factory. Scrap wood accumulates as the window and door frames are produced, and the owner of the business allows the employees to take the discarded wood for use in their fireplaces at home. Bertha's neighbor, Mr. Larson, offers to pay Bertha for fireplace wood and makes it clear that he will not mention the fact that he is paying Bertha for the wood. Bertha reasons that this is OK. She thinks, ''The boss doesn't need to know. Anyway, I'm underpaid on this job, and I can use the extra cash.''

   a.   Do you agree with Bertha's reasoning? Explain your answer.
   b.   Under what circumstances, if any, would you expect Bertha's employer to approve of this arrangement?

15

Moving Ahead in Your Career

LEARNING OBJECTIVES:

1. Develop the ability to adapt to changing job requirements.

2. Set goals for personal and professional growth.

3. Plan and prepare for future job advancement.

4. Explain important considerations in selecting a job.

5. Be sensitive to new developments and plan for retraining and learning new skills.

Jack had been employed for nearly two years working at the counter in an auto parts store. He liked the work, but the challenge was beginning to fade. He became more and more down on his job and began to view his life in general as a dead-end. For a person with ambition and a talent for selling, Jack believed his future in this position was limited. One day Jack shared his feelings with Ilene, the store manager. "I don't feel that I'm getting anywhere in this dumb job," he said. "There are no dumb jobs," Ilene responded, "only dumb people. And you're not one of them. Why don't you get your act together and start moving ahead in a career, instead of being content to

*hustle car parts.'' ''Right!'' said Jack, ''Any suggestions?
You're not doing so bad, Ilene, so why don't you tell me the
secret of your success in this business?''*

___*Your* success identity includes a vision of yourself as a successful worker. The objective of this chapter is to help you develop that vision—to help you plan and prepare for being a winner in your present position and in the various jobs that will become your career ladder. Success in your career consists of discovering your potential and developing it. It includes making the most of what you have to offer an employer, of sharpening your skills and remaining abreast of what is new in your career field—keeping ahead of **obsolescence.** In Chapter 1 you learned that self-fulfillment or **self-actualization** is that for which we all strive. Your self-actualization includes becoming the best that you can be as a worker—moving ahead in your career to reach your full potential.

VISUALIZE SUCCESS IN YOUR CAREER

Why is it important for you to find and move ahead in a career that you like, that you enjoy, and that adds to your success identity? The answer to this question, in part, lies in the number of hours you work in a day. Probably you spend more time on your job than you do in any other one activity. Those hours should be satisfying—adding to your self-fulfillment and contributing to your professional growth. If you are happy during your hours at work, your overall mental and emotional health are enriched. If you are bored, unhappy, or filled with anxiety during those hours, the negative feelings you experience are sure to affect the way you live and work the rest of the day. Furthermore, your hours after work may be filled with activities, that help you escape and forget the negative experiences of the day. On the other hand, if you are happy in your work, you will find that happiness spilling into your hours after work.

DISCOVER YOUR POTENTIAL

The key to success in life, and especially in employment, is to make the best possible use of the things you have going for you. For example, if you

ILLUSTRATION 15-1.
When you are happy in
your hours of work,
your overall mental
and emotional health
are enriched.

are tall, strong, and quick in your physical reactions, you might naturally choose to try out for the basketball team. If your talent is in music and your interest and abilities are not in athletics, you should consider joining the school orchestra. An important reminder here is that you should not undertake something *only* because you have the talent. You must also have an *interest*—a natural desire to participate in the activity. For example, David had talent for music, and early in his life he was encouraged to learn to play the viola. He won young artists' competitions and performed as a soloist with symphony orchestras. Finally, when he was ready for a career as a concert artist, he quit. David simply did not enjoy what he was doing. He had hated the endless hours of practice and the stress of performing before an audience. Finally, following his natural interests and another area of talent, David attended a small university and majored in accounting. Eventually he found self-fulfillment and success in a business career.

If you are to be productive and happy in your work, you must first evaluate your interest and motivation as they relate to employment. Then, with an interesting and challenging occupation in view, you should take an inventory of your employment-related assets. Plan your career development so that you will be able to make the best use of your talents, physical abilities, social skills, and other personal characteristics.

In a consumer economics course, Shelley found a unit on selecting and purchasing a home to be very interesting. As the class worked on a project in which appraisal, negotiating price, mortgage arrangements, and financing were considered, she began to think about real estate selling as a career. But she wondered, "Do I have what it takes to succeed as a real estate salesperson? Are there strengths and weaknesses in my personality, my educational preparation, and my natural abilities that might help or hinder my success?" How might Shelley learn whether this first spark of interest in a real estate career is genuine and realistic?

Now that you are aware of how important it is for you to discover your potential for success in employment, you will want to know how to do it. There are several ways to approach this important task. You may choose to use any or all of them.

Aptitude and Interest Tests

Your school or college counseling office may provide testing services. Probably your community has an employment office which you may use. The names of these offices are different in various parts of the country. Most likely, it is called the Job Service Center. Other names are the Division of Employment and Training, the Human Resources Development Commission, and the Employment Security Office. Most of these agencies participate in employment and testing programs under the supervision of the United States Employment Service.

Testing services can help you in your search for a job to fit your potential. Both seasoned workers and beginning students are assisted in finding the work they can do best. Many of the tests measure characteristics that relate to the demands of various work situations. For instance, do you like detail? You may do well in clerical work. Are you a naturally orderly person? If you are, you have another clue that clerical work may fit your personality. Do you like to solve problems, work with mechanical things, get involved in personal communication with people? Do you enjoy variety and change in your work environment, or do you prefer to work with ideas? All these personal preferences can provide clues about the kinds of occupations in which you are likely to succeed.

In order to take advantage of testing services, you have several choices. One of the best is your local Job Service office. In addition to providing information about employment opportunities, this agency offers testing in the areas of aptitude, interest, temperament, and skills that are critical in matching people with occupations. Modern computer technology makes it possible to compare your individual profile of aptitudes, personality characteristics, and educational qualifications with similar profiles of hundreds of occupations. Therefore, you can identify specific careers that closely match your abilities and interests. The chances for success and personal fulfillment will be greatest for you in these occupations.

Your high school or college job placement or counseling office may have similar testing services for you to use. Also, the information found on the standardized scholastic aptitude tests most high schools use can provide detailed information about occupational fields and levels of ability and aptitude required for success. If you have taken such tests, the information might be available through your school counseling office.

One of the tests that is most often used to evaluate a person's aptitude for various occupations is the General Aptitude Test Battery (GATB). There are no "right" answers for the GATB. You cannot fail this kind of test. Your highest aptitude scores indicate where your greatest potential lies. Given a little help with the interpretation of your profile of aptitude scores, you will be able to visualize your potential clearly. This can provide a solid basis to help expand your self-awareness and self-confidence.

Many other tests, similar to the GATB, but focusing on a specific occupation, are also available. These special aptitude test batteries (in electronics, plumbing, bookkeeping, drafting, auto mechanics, secretarial work, etc.) can give you a more in-depth view of your potential for success in a specific career.

Counseling

Sometimes it helps just to talk to someone about your interests and plans for a career. A teacher, school counselor, employment counselor, relative, or personal friend with whom you feel comfortable can help you explore your interests and abilities as they relate to a career you might be considering. Often just the act of talking with someone can permit you to explore your feelings about yourself. This can help you appreciate the many positive aspects of your personality, your educational and experience qualifications, and your natural abilities. Usually, effective counseling takes more than just one casual conversation. Also, you may want to combine your counseling sessions with other self-exploration activities. This can work to help you more fully appreciate and understand what you have going for you.

ILLUSTRATION 15-2.   Talking to a teacher, school counselor, employment counselor, relative, or personal friend about your interests and plans for a career can be helpful.

Most employment counselors will help you consider whether your interest and temperament qualify you for working mainly with people, with things, or with data. The process should help you recognize a strong interest in mechanics, for instance, or in artistic work. You may say to yourself, "I feel good about myself because I know that I can succeed as a diesel mechanic." or, "I am more sure of myself and optimistic about my chances to succeed as a jewelry designer." At this time your self-image as a person who is talented in some specific area is fresh and new. Next you will want to measure your potential with personal experience.

Hands-On Experiences

The best way to confirm the results of your testing and counseling experiences is to try out what you have learned in the real world of work. Ann's case is a good example. She was pleased but a bit surprised to discover that her mechanical aptitude score on the GATB test was well above her other aptitude scores. She had already made a tentative decision to go into social work as a career—mainly because of the encouragement of her mother, who was employed as a case worker in the county mental health agency.

To test further her mechanical aptitude and her possible interest in mechanical work, Ann spent three days in a career exploration experience arranged by her school counselor. The assignment was to "shadow" a plumber. She observed and assisted him as he went about his work in a new housing development. Ann was fascinated to see how copper pipes were fitted together and sealed with solder. She was given the opportunity to "sweat a joint" herself. The plumber looked carefully for any flaws in the work and found none. He said, "The inspector will approve of this. I'm going to leave it as is instead of doing it over, as I expected when I let you do the job." Ann was delighted. Now she *knew* her mechanical ability was real. She had discovered and measured her potential. Her self-esteem grew and was reflected in an employment interview when she was able to give a strong, positive impression of her potential for success in mechanical work. Eventually, Ann enrolled in a building construction management training program and embarked on a satisfying career that allowed her to make good use of her natural abilities and interests.

Another kind of trial experience that can help you find and confirm your natural abilities and interests is to enroll in a course related to the field you want to explore. Some possibilities are adult education courses, community college or high school classes, apprentice training programs, and instruction sponsored by employers in business and industry. If you do not want to enroll formally in the class, you might talk to the instructor and students. You may be allowed to sit in on a few sessions and look at the course outline or text materials. However, you should be aware that what happens in a class may not be typical of what goes on in the workplace. This is especially true in classes that serve as preparation for more advanced study. For example, a beginning accounting course may not reflect what it is really like to be an accountant. Also, there are many different kinds of jobs (requiring different aptitudes, temperament, etc.) for which accounting graduates may qualify.

Other possibilities exist for testing your interest and ability and for building your self-confidence before you fully commit yourself to a career. Some are career education programs, involvement in vocational student organizations, work experience and cooperative education programs, and actual employment on your own. You may want to try your hand at a number of different kinds of work to see which you find to be most satisfying.

MOVE UP YOUR CAREER LADDER

What you have learned to this point will help you identify realistic, satisfying career goals. But career planning is not something you can do once and for all time. We live in a rapidly changing world, and the changes in the workplace have important messages for you as a worker on the way up.

Remain Flexible

No one can predict what you will be doing three, five, or ten years from now. Changes in the world of work and changes in your own goals and plans are very likely. Therefore, you must expect and plan for change. Of course, you should choose and plan for your success in a career field. Having decided on some general kind of work—something you like, something that matches your interest and ability potential—you must remain flexible. But be ready for change. You may need to retrain, even after you get your job. Some experts say that the job of the future will last only two or three years before the worker will need to learn new skills.

Your goals, then, must be flexible. Moreover, they must be realistic. You must look at your abilities, your interests, your training, your work habits, and your personal qualities with an objective eye.

In setting goals and planning their attainment, you cannot always be definite or specific. You can decide only the direction in which you wish to move. You can be prepared. Many opportunities which you may find cannot be anticipated with exactness. Some element of chance is always present, but you can do much to control your future by training, maintaining a good work record, acquiring a reputation for being highly motivated, being industrious, fitting in and getting along on the job, and being competent. New avenues of opportunity may open for you, and you can be ready. If you are prepared and flexible, you may find employers competing to obtain your services.

Choose Your Jobs Carefully

If you are well qualified, you may have your choice of several positions. You may be hesitant to accept a position that is available because you may think you can find a better position elsewhere. This attitude may or may not be realistic. If you cannot perform your best work with maximum satisfaction in a particular job, you are wise to discover that fact before you begin work. If you are reluctant to accept an available job because your salary or prestige demands are too great, then you may have to adjust your demands. However, as you want to build a satisfying career for yourself, you should not sell yourself short just to obtain immediate employment. Your goal is to market your services for the best possible measure of job stimulation and challenge, security, appreciation, and other rewards.

In deciding whether or not to accept a position, you should consider the following questions:

1. How stable is the firm? Is it just getting started? What are the indications that it will succeed or grow?
2. What opportunities are there for advancement?
3. What promotional policies has the firm established?
4. Will *I* need more education if I remain with the firm? Have I considered plans for such education?
5. When a vacancy occurs in a better position, is someone else likely to be brought into the firm to fill the vacancy?
6. What is the reputation of this firm? within the company itself? among the personnel? among customers or clients? among other people?
7. What security does the position offer? In times of recession, what layoff policy will be followed? Can the employers usually be depended upon to be just and fair? Will the employers keep their word? If sickness takes an employee from work temporarily, will the job be filled by someone else?
8. What kind of retirement plan does the position offer? for unemployment? for sickness and hospitalization and injury?
9. Will the work be challenging enough over a period of years?
10. Do I have the aptitudes, interests, and abilities required by this job?
11. Are there any negative characteristics about the job? (Some people want to avoid night work, travel, or weekend work, for example.)

The best time to plan for advancement is *before* you take a job. One of the considerations you should weigh is the job's promotion possibilities. A well established firm may offer more security than advancement, for example. A new firm, on the other hand, may provide rapid advancement to those employees who are promotion material and yet be less stable than an older firm.

If you are serious about advancement, you should study the possible jobs to which you might be promoted. What other skills, abilities, and traits, in addition to those you now possess, are needed in the new job? Be willing to prepare yourself in these areas before asking for advancement.

Asking for a Raise

The ideal situation exists when true merit is recognized and need never be called to the employer's attention. If your situation is not ideal, what can you do? Obviously, there is only one answer; you must bring the matter up—

you must ask for a raise. Before you speak at all, however, you must think it through very carefully first.

First, see if you are justified in asking for a promotion or a raise. If it appears that you are, make out a good case for yourself *in writing*—but be objective. What about your production? Is there a standard for your work in your position? If so, how does your production compare with this standard? What additional preparation have you made since you were hired? Have you attended extension courses? If you were to take an employment test at this point, could you score higher than on the one you took when you applied for your job?

Next, check your attitudes and work habits. Are you always prompt in arriving for work? Do you work overtime without complaint when it is necessary? How many days of work have you missed because of illness? Are you considered cooperative by your supervisor and your coworkers? When you finish the work assigned, do you find something else to do without being told?

If you feel positive about all these points, then it is time to ask your employer for an appointment. Of course, you may not want to reveal the reason for your request yet. Merely ask for an appointment. (It is a good principle of persuasive psychology to let your employer choose the day and the time.)

If your request for an appointment is granted, bring your notes with you to your interview. You might begin your remarks with something like the following: "Ms. or Mr. Blank, I have enjoyed my work here very much. Since I was hired two years ago, you may be interested in the progress you *have* made." If your statements are challenged, don't back down or get on the defensive. Simply and calmly bring up the case that you have prepared. After all, it is merely another employment interview. Remember—you passed the first one!

Finally, as in other interviews, when you have stated your case, you should thank your employer for the interview and leave. Go back to your work and be patient. Even if your employer has seemed impressed with your facts, you must not expect your raise at once. Your request may be granted after a conference with other members of the firm. Don't ruin a good case by becoming a nuisance. If you hear nothing about your request after two weeks, you might ask your employer if any decision has been made. Both when asking for a raise and following up, keep your tone friendly but impersonal.

Avoid Becoming Obsolete

The first inadequacy you may encounter when you take a new job is in your technical preparation. You may have become proficient on a certain machine, only to discover that your employer has installed another. You may find that the methods, systems, and routines of the new firm are entirely different from those you learned. What should you do?

First of all, keep a learning attitude. No matter how "sold" you may be on the equipment and procedures used in your training or your previous employment, try to adjust to those found in your present job. It will be helpful, also, if you refrain from mentioning how you solved the problem at your former school or on your other job. Like the customer, your boss is always right—at least until you have given the new situation a fair chance.

A learning attitude means that you will be alert for any departure from your present knowledge or training. Suppose your supervisor suggests that you do a certain task in a new way. Pay attention and ask questions if you have any doubts. Write down and number each step of the new method. Ask that it be demonstrated and see if you can follow the demonstration by trying it yourself. Most supervisors prefer spending extra time with new employees rather than having errors appear in their work. Be appreciative of the extra help you receive, too. A considerate employee will find that supervisors will usually respond with equal consideration and will be glad to offer help when needed.

The second type of on-the-job training may be offered to certain employees who have been transferred from other departments, those employees who lack certain needed skills, and those who are expected to work on new equipment or with new procedures. If such training is given you, welcome the opportunity to learn something new. This will set you apart from the other employees, as resistance to change is a common trait. Even if the training involves longer hours, be glad for the opportunity. Learning something new is a guaranteed way of improving your vigor and effectiveness. Take advantage of each opportunity that comes your way.

If, after you have been working in a firm for several years, you should be considered for advancement, you may be asked to take some sort of promotional training. Special training is usually needed before a worker is promoted to a supervisory post. If such an honor should come to you, be aware of the benefits such training will bring you. For example, you may be given help in developing your leadership qualities, in planning your work and the work of others, in developing desirable attitudes, and in evaluating your work and the work of others. This type of training is sure to be helpful to you through all your working life.

Serious Reading

Reading has been an educational tool for thousands of self-made business leaders. Regular reading for short periods of time and on one sub-

ILLUSTRATION 15-3. Reading has been an educational tool for thousands of self-made business leaders.

ject is the secret. If you have not developed the regular reading habit yet, decide to become knowledgeable in some area of interest to you. Get a book or two on the subject from the public library, then start reading. That's all there is to it. It will help if you set aside a special time for general reading of this type. Good reading has a further advantage, too. Writing teachers tell us that the best way to increase your vocabulary is through reading. Such a rewarding activity should not be overlooked.

In case you have no particular interest that you care to pursue, a good start may be made by subscribing to a weekly or monthly magazine devoted to articles of general interest. Another possibility is a subscription to a business periodical. The thing to do is get started. Serious reading is an addictive habit that is good for you! It has been said, by the way, that a mind expanded never returns to its original boundaries.

Educational Courses

In some types of businesses—such as banking and insurance—special courses are offered in community colleges and universities. College credit may be earned if it is desired. These courses provide a splendid opportunity to the ambitious worker, whether a beginner or a long-term employee.

In addition to prescribed courses, you will find adult education classes offered at many high schools as well as universities and colleges. These classes become more popular each year. Many colleges have an extended day enrollment equal to that of their regular programs. The greatest increase is in training for occupations that do not require a four-year degree. One- or two-year programs leading to a certificate or an associate degree are growing in popularity and acceptance. As business continues to emphasize automation, communications, accounting, and overall improved efficiency, education beyond high school becomes more and more essential.

Still another kind of self-improvement study can be pursued through correspondence or home-study courses. These have been discussed in describing job preparation, but they are just as helpful in improving on the job. The major drawback in working by correspondence is that you must motivate yourself. Developing such self-discipline, however, is in itself a valuable accomplishment.

Ability to Change

You are adaptable to change when you are able to adjust, to alter, to fit into, or to respond to changing conditions. Any kind of work in business requires this trait. Your first adaptation must be to your firm. You may have worn sports clothes most of your life, yet you must change willingly to tailored clothes if your firm wishes it.

Second, you need to adapt yourself to the people around you. This includes coworkers, customers, and others with whom you must associate. You may be quick and alert in everything you do or say, yet you must talk slowly and adjust to long pauses if you wish to communicate with someone who thinks, speaks, and reacts slowly. You need to be tolerant of mistaken ideas and refrain from criticism.

A third adjustment must be made to changes in the business world. You will serve your firm best if you are constantly alert to changing routines, to changing conditions of the times, and to the growth and progress of your business. The moods of customers and even the weather may require that you demonstrate your ability to adjust. If you are set in your ways, and cling stubbornly to procedures and methods of the past, you will have failed to develop and practice adaptability. Furthermore, you will be less effective in serving your firm.

IN CONCLUSION

In this chapter you have been encouraged to plan and move ahead in your career. Knowing yourself, taking best advantage of what you have to offer, and establishing yourself in a potentially satisfying career are among the most important tasks you face in life. The suggestions in this chapter are important if you want to be a winner. And, in a larger perspective, the many aspects of personality development presented throughout this book may be the most important preparation you can have for success in the world of work. Before you set this book aside, it might be worth your time to reread the preface. Consider how very important your personality is as a factor in your success on the job. And finally, resolve to be more sensitive about how you should relate to other people so that the best of your personality shows through and works for you.

QUESTIONS AND PROJECTS

1. In accepting a position, what factors, in addition to salary, should be considered?

2. Interview a business executive. Take notes on all that is told you. Ask questions to determine the type of employee wanted by the business.

3. Write down the "case" you would present to your employer when asking for a raise.

4. Interview an experienced worker in a job that you would like to have. Ask this worker to tell you something about the qualities needed for the job, the personality traits that are aids to success, and something about the standards of work.

CASE PROBLEMS

1. It Works Both Ways

Joan is desperate to find a job to support her family. She hears of a job in a box factory and applies at once. She is interviewed by one of the officers and is given a series of tests. The following day, Mrs. Diaz, the person who interviewed Joan, calls her and says she has not been given the job because her test scores were too high. Joan insists that she would be happy to take the job, no matter what the test scores say. Mrs. Diaz insists, however, that it is company policy to give routine, repetitive jobs only to applicants of average ability. Joan feels that she has been treated unfairly.

a. Why should such a policy be made? What is its purpose?

   b. Do you agree that Joan might not enjoy working at repetitive, monotonous work?
   c. What should Joan do now? Is there any place she can go for further advice?
   d. What other policies can you suggest for dealing with this problem of repetition?

2. Time for Decision.

Russ Palmer has been working in the programming department of White and Charters, Inc., since he graduated from junior college a year ago. Since the time he began working with the firm, he has received no raises in salary. The work of the programming department, however, has increased to the extent that two new employees have been hired to help him. This involves some supervisory work on his part. In checking the salaries paid by other firms for similar work, Russ finds that he is not earning as much as other companies pay. As Russ is debating what to do, a friend who is office manager of Hanson and Hanson Company offers him the same type of job at 15 percent higher salary. Russ likes the people in his department as well as the other personnel at White and Charters. Hanson and Hanson do not provide the fringe benefits he is receiving.

a. What would you do if you were Russ?
b. If you decide to ask for a raise, would you tell your employer about the offer?

Index

FEB 0 9 1990	DATE DUE	
2-23		
FEB 2 4 1995		

LIBRARY

EASTERN OREGON STATE COLLEGE

LA GRANDE, OREGON